THE BRITANNICA GUIDE TO THE SOCIAL SCIENCES

SOCIOLOGY

EDITED BY

STEPHANIE J. ALEXANDER

Educational Publishing

IN ASSOCIATION WITH

ROSEN

EDUCATIONAL SERVICES

Published in 2016 by Britannica Educational Publishing (a trademark of Encyclopædia Britannica, Inc.) in association with The Rosen Publishing Group, Inc.
29 East 21st Street, New York, NY 10010

Distributed exclusively by Rosen Publishing.

To see additional Britannica Educational Publishing titles, go to rosenpublishing.com.

First Edition

Britannica Educational Publishing
J.E. Luebering: Director, Core Reference Group
Anthony L. Green: Editor, Compton's by Britannica

Rosen Publishing
Christine Poolos: Editor
Nelson Sá: Art Director
Brian Garvey: Designer
Cindy Reiman: Photography Manager
Bruce Donnola: Photo Researcher

Library of Congress Cataloging-in-Publication Data

Sociology
Sociology / edited by Stephanie J. Alexander.
pages cm. — (The Britannica guide to the social sciences)
Includes bibliographical references and index.
ISBN 978-1-62275-555-4 (library bound)
1. Sociology—Juvenile literature. I. Alexander, Stephanie J. II. Title.
HM585.S61586 2016
301—dc23

2015018954

Manufactured in the United States of America

Photo credits: Cover, p. 1 marigold_88/iStock/Thinkstock; p. xii H. Roger-Viollet; pp. 2, 48 Universal Images Group/Getty Images; pp. 5, 9, 43 Photos.com/Thinkstock; pp. 13, 19 ullstein bild/Getty Images; p. 25 Blend Images/SuperStock; p. 27 Joseph Sohm/Shutterstock.com; p. 30 paul prescott/Shutterstock.com; p. 32 Chris Jackson/Getty Images; p. 40 Ed Giles/Getty Images; p. 55 © North Wind Picture Archives; p. 57 Photos.com/Jupiterimages; p. 62 Leif Geiges; p. 72 Bibliotheque Nationale, Paris, France/Bridgeman Images; p. 75 Photo © PVDE/Bridgeman Images; p. 81 Pictorial Parade/Archive Photos/Getty Images; p. 88 Leonard McCombe/The LIFE Images Collection/Getty Images; p. 90 Archive Photos/Getty Images; p. 91 Ted Thai/The LIFE Images Collection/Getty Images; p. 99 John G. White/The Denver Post/Getty Images; p. 111 © INTERFOTO/Alamy; p. 116 George Pimentel/Getty Images; pp. 120-121 Private Collection/© Look and Learn/Bridgeman Images; p. 121 Jay Paull/Archive Photos/Getty Images; p. 124 © DPA/Courtesy Everett Collection; p. 132 Barcroft/Getty Images

CONTENTS

Introduction vi

Chapter One
What Are the Social Sciences? 1
The 19th Century 1
Resulting Major Themes 3
Thomas Malthus 4
Charles Cooley 7
New Intellectual and
Philosophical Tendencies 10
Sociology as a Separate Discipline 12
The 20th Century 17
Marxist Influences 18
Freudian Influences 19
Specialization and Cross-Disciplinary
Approaches 20
Theoretical Modes 21

Chapter Two
What Is Sociology? 25
Society and Social Structure 26
Social Movements 28
Structure and Social Organization ... 30
Social Status 31
Castes 33
Social Change 35

Chapter Three
The Origins of Sociology 42
August Comte 42
Harriet Martineau 45
Founding the Discipline 47
Herbert Spencer 48

2

30

43

E.B. Tylor 50
Individualism 51
Lewis Henry Morgan 54
Leonard Hobhouse 56
Social Darwinism 56

Chapter Four
Early Sociological Theories 59
Econmic Determinism 59
Human Ecology 61
Social Psychology 63
Cultural Theory 69
Early Schools of Thought 70
Early Functionalism 70
Emile Durkheim 73
The Functionalist-Conflict Debate ... 74
Structural Functionalism 76
Theories of Class and Power 77
Talcott Parsons 78
Structuralism 80
The Frankfurt School 82
Rising Segmentation of the Discipline 84

Chapter Five
Major Modern Developments 85
Social Stratification 85
C. Wright Mills 87
Social Class 90
William Julius Wilson 92
Interdisciplinary Influences 95
The Historical Divide: Qualitative and Establishment Sociology 97
James S. Coleman 98

Chapter Six
Methodological Considerations in Sociology 102
Methodological Development in Contemporary Sociology 104
Florian Znaniecki 105
Ecological Patterning 106
William Fielding Ogburn 107
Howard W. Odum 109
Experiments 110
Statistics and Mathematical Analysis 111
Sociometry 113
Data Collection 114
National Methodological Preferences .. 115

Chapter Seven
The Status of Contemporary Sociology 118
Academic Status 118
Albion Small 119
Louis Wirth 122
Scientific Status 127
Robert Park 129
Current Trends 130
Emerging Roles for Sociologists 133

Conclusion 134
Glossary 135
Bibliography 138
Index 140

111

120

132

INTRODUCTION

The study of human behaviour in social groups is called sociology. This social science tries to describe everything about a society or social subgroup that gives it special characteristics distinct from other groups. The actions of animals are based mainly on instinct. Human behaviour, by contrast, seems to be shaped and conditioned by interactions among persons and groups. Sociology therefore includes the study of customs, traditions, patterns of historical development, and institutions that have emerged within specific societies. A social institution is a group organization or custom such as marriage, family, ways of holding property, educational arrangements, government, or legal system.

Within any population the smallest social unit is the family. It is therefore possible to develop a sociology of the family within a given society. There are also branches of sociology devoted to studying poverty, religion, the working class, women, immigrants, ethnic groups, teenagers, criminals, and other units. Whatever the unit, a study seeks to describe and explain the behaviour of people within the group on the basis of their distinctive customs and their interactions.

Sociology looks at how groups of people are similar and how they differ from each other. Since the 1970s, for example, there have been several studies comparing industrial workers in the United States with those in Japan—trying to account for varying levels of productivity, different attitudes toward work, and different relationships to the workplace. Other studies investigate ways in which family structure among immigrants differs from family structure typical of their country of origin.

GOALS AND METHODS

Ever since sociology emerged as a scientific discipline in the late 19th century, its purposes have been disputed. Some scholars maintain that its goal is simply to understand the nature and behaviour of social groups. Others contend that the purpose of study is to cause social change—to make sociology an instrument for the improvement of the human environment. The question became: Is sociology descriptive only, or should it also be normative—presenting the standards by which change is to be measured?

The methods involved in sociological analysis are some of the same ones used in other sciences. Among them are observation, statistical measurement, data collection, experimentation, and the examination of human ecology. The chief problem in all methods is controlling the variables. It is easier to study animals and plants than human beings because plant and animal behaviours can be controlled and monitored—and they are predictable. Human behaviour, in individuals or in groups, is not predictable—nor can it be easily controlled. Many more variables are found in sociological research than are seen in a chemistry or biology laboratory.

OBSERVATION

Observation, or field research, is a basic means of collecting information. It means putting oneself within a social group to see how it functions, what its institutions are, and what values it cherishes. Herbert Gans published such a study in 1962. Entitled *The Urban Villagers*, it was a careful examination of the Italian Americans of Boston's West End.

STATISTICAL METHODS

Statistical methods were introduced into sociology from other disciplines quite early and helped establish it as a science. The gathering of statistics proved useful in measuring trends, changes, attitudes, and other characteristics of a society. The use of statistics as a means to analyze society dates back to the 17th century. Edmond Halley, among others, used what was called political arithmetic to create mortality tables. Some analysts used birth and death rates to ascertain how rapidly the population of London recovered from the effects of the Great Plague of 1664–66. In France the statesman Jean-Baptiste Colbert ordered the keeping of parish records and of yearly data on marriages, births, and deaths.

DATA COLLECTION

Data collection for sociological research is done in a variety of ways, all somewhat unreliable, as allowances must be made for bias. Two common methods of data collection are the interview and the questionnaire. In both cases the questions must be comprehensible to the least-educated persons within the subject population. Questions must be meaningful to individuals of differing backgrounds; they must avoid topics that are likely to arouse resistance or hostility; and they must be precisely worded in order to avoid wide variations in the answers.

EXPERIMENTS

Experiments in social interaction are usually conducted in artificial situations, frequently laboratories and classrooms. Small-group research, such as the group dynamics sessions founded by social psychologist Kurt Lewin, produces tentative results because the participants normally know in advance they are part of an experiment. Success in experiments is usually greatest in simple situations in which the number of variables has been minimized.

ECOLOGICAL METHODS

Ecological methods of sociological research were developed in urban studies. Research on cities consists in part of mapping the distribution of population with regard to ethnicity, business and industry, and certain behaviour patterns—for example, family disorganization, mental disorders, crime and delinquency, and vice. All of these were shown to be part of a general urban ecology, and it has become possible through ecological mapping to pinpoint the sociological characteristics of a geographic area.

RELATED FIELDS

Because sociology focuses on all the characteristics of a human society, it has considerable overlap with other disciplines. Four closely related fields in the social sciences are anthropology, criminology, demography, and social psychology.

ANTHROPOLOGY

The word "anthropology" comes from the Greek and means the "study of humans." It is often subdivided into cultural anthropology and physical anthropology. Cultural anthropology is concerned with the growth of human society—group behaviour, the origins of religions, social customs and conventions, technical developments, and family relationships.

Physical anthropology deals with the biological aspects of humans—racial differences, human origins, and evolution. The goals of anthropologists are much the same as those of sociologists, but the means they use are different. Anthropology in its study of modern cultures uses direct observation of human beings, their activities, and their products. The study of past societies is dependent on the work of archaeologists because it needs artifacts—pottery, weapons, fabrics, and other objects—as well as skeletal remains of the people as evidence for its findings. Some anthropologists study surviving preliterate societies.

CRIMINOLOGY

Criminology is the scientific study of the causes of crime and how it may be prevented. It is basically a subfield of sociology, but it has grown so large that it is usually treated as a separate course in higher education. It originated in the 18th century, when controversy arose between those who wanted to use prisons and punishments for reform and deterrence and those who insisted that punishment should include retribution. In the 19th century one school of criminology insisted that criminals are shaped by their environments and thus should be given the chance for rehabilitation. An opposite school denied this view and claimed that the rights of criminals must be balanced by the rights of society.

DEMOGRAPHY

Demography studies the distribution of population by age, sex, marital status, and other characteristics. It also focuses on population changes—movement from place to place, trends in fertility rates, and birth and death rates. One emphasis relates population size to the potential for economic growth. The term "population explosion," for example, suggests that a given society may become too large to be fed, clothed, and housed by its resources. Other aspects of demography examine problems of urban congestion, illegal immigration, and the size of the labor force in relation to employment potential.

Although the word "demography" was not in use until about 1880, the science originated in the second half of the 17th century with the work of John Graunt in London. He studied weekly birth and death records for the century and created the first mortality table. In the next century a German, Johann Süssmilch, used similar statistical materials to construct a mortality table for all of Prussia. (Mortality tables summarize the life spans of individuals within a given population. They are used by insurance companies as a statistical device to calculate premiums on the basis of projected life span.) Demographic studies today are based primarily on censuses and the registration of vital statistics (births and deaths).

SOCIAL PSYCHOLOGY

Social psychology is the scientific study of individual behaviour in a social and cultural setting. Its concern is the effect of society on the personality, motivations, and attitudes of the individual. Social psychologists seek to answer such questions as: How are children affected when both parents work? What is the impact of the assembly line on the mental and emotional makeup of industrial workers? What effects do mass media have on political and social attitudes?

HISTORICAL BACKGROUND OF SOCIOLOGY

The word "sociology" was coined by French philosopher Auguste Comte in 1837. Up to that time the subject matter of sociology had belonged to philosophy. Ancient literature contained many brilliant insights concerning group life, social organization, and interpersonal relations.

Auguste Comte

Systematic thought on society was begun by the Greek philosophers, especially Plato and Aristotle. But they and their followers for many centuries persisted in identifying society with the political order. It was an easy mistake to make because the people who really mattered—so it was thought—were the rulers, soldiers, and priests who made up society's command structures. Not until the late 18th century did philosophers begin to make a clear distinction between society and its political form. The chief early representative of this shift in emphasis was the French writer Jean-Jacques Rousseau in such books as *The Social Contract* and *Discourse on the Origin of Inequality*.

Because Comte coined the term, he is called the father of sociology. He conceived of it as a general social science that—like philosophy—would bring together all knowledge about humanity. It was left to later writers to define sociology as a field distinct from other social sciences. Four of the most influential in doing this were Émile Durkheim, Max Weber, Charles Horton Cooley, and Albion Small.

If someone other than Comte can be considered the founder of sociology, it is probably Durkheim. He stated that sociology should be a discipline devoted solely to the study of "social facts." These facts include forms of behaviour, thought, and feeling and are to be studied as collective characteristics of a society, not as individual manifestations.

Weber viewed sociology as a science for understanding and interpreting social behaviour in order to predict future behaviour. He recognized the usefulness of statistics. His research on bureaucracy and social stratification contributed significantly to the ongoing investigation of these subjects.

Cooley's major contribution was in making human ecology a field of sociology. His definitions of primary group, the looking-glass self, communication, and the relation of society to the individual gave future sociologists much of their conceptual framework.

Small, as a professor at the University of Chicago, helped make sociology a distinct academic course and a profession. He introduced European sociological thought into the United States. With George E.

Vincent he wrote *An Introduction to the Study of Society* (1894), which was the first sociology textbook in the United States.

Beginning in the last quarter of the 19th century, sociology quickly established itself in the colleges and universities of the United States. The subject matter of sociology was often combined with other courses—usually history or politics—and the teachers remained mainly social philosophers. The first course actually called sociology was taught at Yale University in 1876 by William Graham Sumner. By 1892 sociology was taught at 18 colleges and universities. In that year Small arrived at the then new University of Chicago and was given the responsibility of establishing a department of sociology—the first such department in the world. Other departments were soon established at Columbia, the universities of Kansas and Michigan; and at Yale and Brown. By the end of the century nearly all colleges and universities had departments, or at least courses, in sociology.

The *American Journal of Sociology* began publication at the University of Chicago in 1895. The school would long remain one of the world's leading centers in the subject. Over the years the strong faculty included George H. Mead, William I. Thomas, and Ellsworth Farris. The American Sociological Society, founded in 1905, was the predecessor of many regional, national, international, and specialized sociological organizations. The International Sociological Association was founded in 1949.

This resource will first provide a broader background of the social sciences, of which sociology is a part. It will then explain the discipline of sociology itself, examining its origins and development, including pioneering social scientists and their theories. Finally, it will take a look at the methodology used by sociologists and developments in the field today.

CHAPTER ONE

WHAT ARE THE SOCIAL SCIENCES?

Sociology is part of the broad discipline known as the social sciences. These also include cultural (or social) anthropology, social psychology, political science, economics, social and economic geography, and those areas of education that deal with the social contexts of learning and the relation of the school to the social order. The social sciences deal with human behaviour in its social and cultural aspects. While they are separate studies, the disciplines within the social sciences have much in common, including theories, history, and influences.

Although, strictly speaking, sociology and the social sciences do not precede the 19th century—that is, as distinct and recognized disciplines of thought—one can go back farther in time for the origins of some of their fundamental ideas and objectives. In the largest sense, the origins go all the way back to the ancient Greeks and their rationalist inquiries into the nature of humans, the state, and morality. The heritage of both Greece and Rome is a powerful one in the history of social thought, as it is in other areas of Western society. Very probably, apart from the initial Greek determination to study all things in the spirit of dispassionate and rational inquiry, there would be no social sciences and no sociology today.

THE 19TH CENTURY

The fundamental ideas, themes, and problems of sociology and the rest of the social sciences in the 19th century are best understood as responses to the problem of order that was created in people's minds by the weakening of the old order, or European society, under the twin blows of the French Revolution and the Industrial Revolution. The breakup of the old order—an order that had rested on kinship, land, social class, religion, local community, and monarchy—set free, as it were, the complex elements of status, authority, and wealth that had been for so long consolidated. In the same way that the history of 19th-century politics, industry, and trade is basically about the practical efforts of human beings to reconsolidate these elements, so the history of 19th-century social thought is about theoretical efforts to reconsolidate them—that is, to give them new contexts of meaning.

In terms of the immediacy and sheer massiveness of impact on human thought and values, it would be difficult to find revolutions

The Industrial Revolution brought about far-reaching changes to the structure and order of society.

of comparable magnitude in human history. The political, social, and cultural changes that began in France and England at the very end of the 18th century spread almost immediately through Europe and the Americas in the 19th century and then on to Asia, Africa, and the island states and territories of the Pacific Ocean in the 20th century. The effects of the two revolutions, the one overwhelmingly democratic in thrust, the other industrial-capitalist, have been to undermine, shake, or topple institutions that had endured for centuries, even millennia, and with them systems of authority, status, belief, and community.

The coining or redefining of words is an excellent indication of people's perceptions of change in a given historical period. A large number of words taken for granted today came into being in the period marked by the final decade or two of the 18th century and the first quarter of the 19th. Among these are: industry, industrialist, democracy, class, middle class, ideology, intellectual, rationalism, humanitarian, atomistic, masses, commercialism, proletariat, collectivism, equalitarian, liberal, conservative, scientist, utilitarian, bureaucracy, capitalism, and crisis. Some of these words were invented; others reflect new and very different meanings given to old ones. All alike bear witness to the transformed character of the European social landscape as this landscape loomed up to the leading minds of the age. And all these words bear witness too to the emergence of new social philosophies and, most pertinent to the subject of this article, the social sciences as they are known today.

RESULTING MAJOR THEMES

It is illuminating to mention a few of the major themes in social thought in the 19th century that were almost the direct results of the democratic and industrial revolutions. It should be borne in mind that these themes are to be seen in the philosophical and literary writing of the age as well as in social thought.

First, there was the great increase in population. Between 1750 and 1850 the population of Europe went from 140,000,000 to 266,000,000;

in the world from 728,000,000 to well over 1,000,000,000. It was an English clergyman-economist, Thomas Malthus, who, in his famous work *An Essay on the Principle of Population*, first marked the enormous significance to human welfare of this increase. With the diminution of historic checks on population growth, chiefly those of high mortality rates—a diminution that was, as Malthus realized, one of the rewards of technical progress—there were no easily foreseeable limits to growth of population. And such growth, he stressed, could only upset the traditional balance between population and food supply. Not all social

Thomas Malthus

The reputation of the English economist Thomas Robert Malthus endured because of his work *An Essay on the Principle of Population*, published in 1798. In it he sought to show that increases in population will eventually diminish the ability of the world to feed itself. He based this conclusion on the thesis that populations expand in such a way as to overtake the possibility of adding enough land for crops. While some of Malthus' assertions have been discounted by many economists, 20th-century concerns over population growth brought him back into favour.

Malthus was born in Rookery, Surrey, in February 1766. He attended Cambridge University, earning a master's degree in 1791. In 1805 he became professor of history and political economy at the East India Company's college in Haileybury, Hertfordshire, and he remained there the rest of his life. He died on Dec. 29, 1834, in St. Catherine, near Bath, Somerset, Eng.

Malthus was a pessimist who viewed the popular notion of human perfectibility as foolishness. As he continued studying economics, he became concerned with problems of supply and demand, gluts of goods, and recessions. Many of his ideas anticipated the thinking of John Maynard Keynes a century later.

Thomas Malthus

scientists in the century took the pessimistic view of the matter that Malthus did but few if any were indifferent to the impact of explosive increase in population on economy, government, and society.

Second, there was the condition of labour. It may be possible to see this condition in the early 19th century as in fact better than the condition of the rural masses at earlier times. But the important point is that to a large number of writers in the 19th century it seemed worse and was defined as worse. The wrenching of large numbers of people from the older and protective contexts of village, guild, parish, and family, and their massing in the new centres of industry, forming slums, living in common squalor and wretchedness, their wages generally behind cost of living, their families growing larger, their standard of living becoming lower, as it seemed—all of this is a frequent theme in the social thought of the century.

Third, there was the transformation of property. Not only was more and more property to be seen as industrial—manifest in the factories, business houses, and workshops of the period—but also the very nature of property was changing. Whereas for most of the history of humankind property had been "hard," visible only in concrete possessions—land and money—now the more intangible kinds of property such as shares of stock, negotiable equities of all kinds, and bonds were assuming ever greater influence in the economy. This led, as was early realized, to the dominance of financial interests, to speculation, and to a general widening of the gulf between the propertied and the masses. The change in the character of property made easier the concentration of property, the accumulation of immense wealth in the hands of a relative few, and, not least, the possibility of economic domination of politics and culture.

Fourth, there was urbanization—the sudden increase in the number of towns and cities in western Europe and the increase in number of persons living in the historic towns and cities. Whereas in earlier centuries, the city had been regarded almost uniformly as a setting of civilization, culture, and freedom of mind, now one found more and more writers aware of the other side of cities: the atomization of human relationships,

Charles Cooley

Charles Horton Cooley (1864–1929) was a U.S. sociologist who employed a sociopsychological approach to the understanding of society. He earned his Ph.D. at the University of Michigan in 1894. He had started teaching at the university in 1892, became a full professor of sociology in 1907, and remained there until the end of his life.

Cooley believed that social reality was qualitatively different from physical reality and was therefore less amenable to measurement. Because of this view, he was more productive as a social theorist than as a research scientist. His *Human Nature and the Social Order* (1902, reprinted 1956) discussed the determination of the self through interaction with others. Cooley theorized that the sense of self is formed in two ways: by one's actual experiences and by what one imagines others' ideas of oneself to be—a phenomenon Cooley called the "looking glass self." This dual conception contributed to Cooley's fundamental theory that the mind is social and that society is a mental construct.

In *Social Organization* (1909, reprinted 1956), Cooley outlined the objective consequences of his psychological views. He argued that the ideal of the moral unity of society, involving qualities of loyalty, justice, and freedom, was derived from face-to-face relationships in primary groups such as the family and neighbourhood or children's play groups. In his last major work, *Social Process* (1918, reprinted 1966), he applied the Darwinian principles of natural selection and adaptation to collective (social) existence.

broken families, the sense of the mass, of anonymity, alienation, and disrupted values. Sociology particularly among the social sciences turned its attention to the problems of urbanization. The contrast between the more organic type of community found in rural areas and the more mechanical and individualistic society of the cities is a basic contrast in sociology, one that was given much attention by such pioneers in Europe as the French sociologists Frédéric Le Play and Émile Durkheim; the German sociologists Ferdinand Tönnies, Georg Simmel, and Max Weber; the Belgian statistician Adolphe Quetelet; and, in America, by the sociologists Charles H. Cooley and Robert E. Park.

Fifth, there was technology. With the spread of mechanization, first in the factories, then in agriculture, social thinkers could see possibilities of a rupture of the historic relations between human beings and nature, between human beings themselves, even between humanity and God. To thinkers as politically different as Thomas Carlyle and Karl Marx, technology seemed to lead to dehumanization of the worker and to exercise of a new kind of tyranny over human life. Marx, though, far from despising technology, thought the advent of socialism would counteract all this. Alexis de Tocqueville declared that technology, and especially technical specialization of work, was more degrading to the human mind and spirit than even political tyranny. It was thus in the 19th century that the opposition to technology on moral, psychological, and aesthetic grounds first made its appearance in Western thought.

Sixth, there was the factory system. Along with urbanization and spreading mechanization, the system of work whereby masses of workers left home and family to work long hours in the factories became a major theme of social thought as well as of social reform.

Seventh, and finally, mention is to be made of the development of political masses—that is, the slow but inexorable widening of franchise and electorate through which ever larger numbers of persons became aware of themselves as voters and participants in the political process. Tocqueville saw the rise of the political masses, more especially the immense power that could be wielded by the masses, as the

Karl Marx

single greatest threat to individual freedom and cultural diversity in the ages ahead.

These, then, are the principal themes in the 19th-century writing that may be seen as direct results of the two great revolutions. As themes, they are to be found not only in the social sciences but, as noted above, in a great deal of the philosophical and literary writing of the century. In their respective ways, the philosophers Hegel, Coleridge, and Emerson were as struck by the consequences of the revolutions as were any social scientists. So too were such novelists as Balzac and Dickens.

NEW INTELLECTUAL AND PHILOSOPHICAL TENDENCIES

It is important also to identify three other powerful tendencies of thought that influenced all of the social sciences. The first is a positivism that was not merely an appeal to science but almost reverence for science; the second, humanitarianism; the third, the philosophy of evolution.

The positivist appeal of science was to be seen everywhere. The 19th century saw the virtual institutionalization of the ideal of science. The great aim was that of dealing with moral values, institutions, and all social phenomena through the same fundamental methods that could be seen so luminously in such areas as physics and biology. Prior to the 19th century, no very clear distinction had been made between philosophy and science, and the term "philosophy" was even preferred by those working directly with physical materials, seeking laws and principles in the fashion of a Newton or Harvey—that is, by persons whom one would now call scientists.

In the 19th century, in contrast, the distinction between philosophy and science became an overwhelming one. Virtually every area of human thought and behaviour was thought by a rising number of persons to be amenable to scientific investigation in precisely the same degree that physical data were. More than anyone else, it was Comte who heralded the idea of the scientific treatment of social behaviour. His *Cours de philosophie positive*, published in six volumes between 1830 and 1842, sought to demonstrate irrefutably not merely the possibility but the inevitability of a human science, one for which Comte coined the word "sociology" and that would do for humans a social beings exactly what biology had already done for humans as biological animals. But Comte was far from alone. There were many in the century to join in his celebration of science for the study of society.

Humanitarianism, though a very distinguishable current of thought in the century, was closely related to the idea of a science of society. For the ultimate purpose of social science and in particular sociology was thought by almost everyone to be the welfare of society, the improvement of its moral and social condition. Humanitarianism, strictly defined, is the institutionalization of compassion; it is the extension of welfare from the limited areas in which these had historically been found, chiefly family and village, to society at large. One of the most notable and also distinctive aspects of the 19th century was the constantly rising number of persons, almost wholly from the middle class, who worked directly for the betterment of society. In the many projects and proposals for relief of the destitute, improvement of slums, amelioration of the plight of the insane, the indigent, and imprisoned, and other afflicted minorities could be seen the spirit of humanitarianism at work. All kinds of associations were formed, including temperance associations, groups and societies for the abolition of slavery and of poverty and for the improvement of literacy, among other objectives.

The third of the intellectual influences is that of evolution. It affected every one of the social sciences. An interest in development was to be found in the 18th century, as noted earlier. But this interest was small and specialized compared with 19th-century theories of social evolution. The impact of Charles Darwin's *On the Origin of Species*, published in 1859, was of course great and further enhanced the appeal of the evolutionary view of things. But it is very important to recognize that ideas of social evolution had their own origins and contexts. The evolutionary works of such social scientists as Comte, Herbert Spencer, and Marx had been completed, or well begun, before publication of Darwin's work. The important point, in any event, is that the idea or the philosophy of evolution was in the air throughout the century, as profoundly contributory to the establishment of sociology as a systematic discipline in the 1830s as to such fields as geology, astronomy, and biology.

SOCIOLOGY AS A SEPARATE DISCIPLINE

Among the disciplines that formed the social sciences, two contrary, for a time equally powerful, tendencies at first dominated them. The first was the drive toward unification, toward a single, master social science, whatever it might be called. The second tendency was toward specialization of the individual social sciences.

When, in the 1820s, Comte wrote calling for a new science, one with humans as social animals as the subject, he assuredly had but a single, encompassing science of society in mind—not a congeries of disciplines, each concerned with some single aspect of human behaviour in society. The same was true of Bentham, Marx, and Spencer. All these minds, and there were many others to join them, saw the study of society as a unified enterprise. They would have scoffed, and on occasion did, at any notion of a separate economics, political science, sociology, and so on. Society is an indivisible thing, they would have argued; so, too, must be the study of society.

It was, however, the opposite tendency of specialization or differentiation that won out. No matter how the century began, or what were the dreams of a Comte, Spencer, or Marx, when the 19th century ended not one but several distinct, competitive social sciences were to be found. Aiding this process was the development of the colleges and universities. With hindsight it might be said that the cause of universities in the future would have been strengthened, as would the cause of

Herbert Spencer

the social sciences, had there come into existence, successfully, a single curriculum, undifferentiated by field, for the study of society. What in fact happened, however, was the opposite. The growing desire for an elective system, for a substantial number of academic specializations, and for differentiation of academic degrees, contributed strongly to the differentiation of the social sciences.

By the end of the 19th century all the major social sciences had achieved a distinctiveness, an importance widely recognized, and were, especially in the cases of economics and political science, fully accepted as disciplines in the universities. Most important, they were generally accepted as sciences in their own right rather than as minions of philosophy. It was economics that first attained the status of a single and separate science, in ideal at least, among the social sciences. Rivalling economics as a discipline during the century was political science. There was a strong interest, especially in the late 19th century, in the origins of political institutions in kinship, village, and caste, and in the successive stages of development that have characterized these institutions. In political science, as in economics, in short, the classical analytical approach was strongly rivalled by the evolutionary. In the 19th century, anthropology also attained clear identity as a discipline. Strictly defined as "the science of man," it could be seen as superseding other specialized disciplines such as economics and political science. In practice and from the beginning, however, anthropology concerned itself overwhelmingly with small-scale preindustrial societies. From cultural anthropology more than from any other single social science has come the emphasis on the cultural foundations of man's behaviour and thought in society. Social psychology as a distinct discipline also originated in the 19th century, although its outlines were perhaps somewhat less clear than was true of the other social sciences. The close relation of the human mind to the social order, its dependence upon education and other forms of socialization, was well known in the 18th century. Although the point of departure in each of the studies was the nature of association, they dealt, in one degree or other, with the internal processes of psychosocial interaction, the operation of attitudes and judgments, and the social basis of personality and thought—in short, with those phenomena that would, at least in the 20th century, be the substance of social psychology as a formal discipline. Two final manifestations of the social sciences in the 19th century are social statistics and social (or human) geography. And both were to exert a great deal of influence on the other social sciences by the beginning of the 20th century: social statistics on sociology and social psychology pre-eminently; social geography on political science, economics, history, and certain areas of anthropology, especially those areas dealing with the dispersion of races and the diffusion of cultural elements.

During much of the 19th century it was not easy to distinguish between a great deal of so-called sociology and social or cultural anthropology. Even if almost no sociologists in the century made empirical studies of primitive peoples, as did the anthropologists, their interest in the origin, development, and probable future of humankind was not less great than what could be found in the writings of the anthropologists. It was Auguste Comte who coined the word "sociology," and he used it to refer to what he imagined would be a single, all-encompassing science of society that would take its place at the top of the hierarchy of sciences—a hierarchy that Comte saw as including astronomy (the oldest of the sciences historically) at the bottom and with physics, chemistry, and biology rising in that order to sociology, the latest and grandest of the sciences. There was no thought in Comte's mind—nor was there in the mind of Herbert Spencer, whose general view of sociology was very much like Comte's—of there being other, competing social sciences. Sociology would be to the whole of the social world what each of the other great sciences was to its appropriate sphere of reality.

Both Comte and Spencer believed that civilization as a whole was the proper subject of sociology. Their works were concerned, for the most part, with describing the origins and development of civilization and also of each of its major institutions. Both declared sociology's main divisions to be "statics" and "dynamics," the former concerned with processes of order in society, the latter with processes of evolutionary change in society. Both thinkers also saw all existing societies in the world as reflective of the successive stages through which Western society had advanced in time over a period of tens of thousands of years.

Not all sociologists in the 19th century conceived their discipline in this light, however. Side by side with the "grand" view represented by Comte and Spencer were those who were primarily interested in the social problems that they saw around them—consequences, as they interpreted them, of the two revolutions, the industrial and democratic. Thus in France just after midcentury, Frédéric Le Play published a monumental study of the social aspects of the working classes in Europe, *Les Ouvriers européens* ("European Workers"), which compared families and communities in all parts of Europe and even other parts of the world. Alexis de Tocqueville, especially in the second volume of his *Democracy in America* (1835), provided an account of the customs, social structures, and institutions in America, dealing with these—and also with the social and psychological problems of Americans in that day—as aspects of the impact of the democratic and industrial revolutions upon traditional society.

At the very end of the 19th century, in both France and Germany, there appeared some of the works in sociology that were to prove more influential in their effects upon the discipline in the 20th century. Ferdinand Tönnies, in his *Gemeinschaft und Gesellschaft* (1887; *Community and Society*), sought to explain all major social problems in the West as the consequence of the historical transition from the communal, status-based, concentric society of the Middle Ages to the more individualistic, impersonal, and large-scale society of the democratic-industrial period. In general terms, allowing for individual variations of theme, these were the views of Max Weber, Georg Simmel, and Émile Durkheim (all of whom also wrote in the late 19th and early 20th century). These were the researchers who, starting from the problems of

Western society that could be traced to the effects of the two revolutions, did the most to establish the discipline of sociology as it was practiced for much of the 20th century.

THE 20TH CENTURY

In the 20th century, the processes first generated by the democratic and industrial revolutions proceeded virtually unchecked in Western society, penetrating more and more spheres of once traditional morality and culture, leaving their impress on more and more nations, regions, and localities. Equally important, perhaps in the long run far more so, was the spread of these revolutionary processes to non-Western areas of the world. The impact of industrialism, technology, secularism, and individualism upon peoples long accustomed to the ancient unities of tribe, local community, agriculture, and religion was first to be seen in the context of colonialism, an outgrowth of nationalism and capitalism in the West. The relations of the West to non-Western parts of the world, the whole phenomenon of the "new nations," represented vital aspects of the social sciences.

So too were certain other consequences, or lineal episodes, of the two revolutions. The 20th century was the century of nationalism, mass democracy, large-scale industrialism, and developments in communication and information technology beyond the reach of any 19th-century imagination so far as magnitude is concerned. It was also the century of mass warfare, of two world wars with tolls in lives and property greater perhaps than the sum total of all preceding wars in history. It was the century too of totalitarianism: communist, fascist, and Nazi; and of techniques of terrorism that, if not novel, reached a scale and an intensity of scientific application that could scarcely have been predicted by those who considered science and technology as unqualifiedly humane in possibility. It was a century of affluence in the West, without precedent for the masses of people, evidenced in a constantly rising standard of living and a constantly rising level of expectations.

The last is important. A great deal of the turbulence in the 20th century—political, economic, and social—resulted from desires and aspirations that had been constantly escalating and that had been passing from relatively homogenous groups in the West to ethnic and racial minorities among them and, then, to whole continents elsewhere. Of all manifestations of revolution, the revolution of rising expectations is perhaps the most powerful in its consequences. For, once this revolution gets under way, each fresh victory in the struggle for rights, freedom, and security tends to magnify the importance of what has not been won.

Once it was thought that, by solving the fundamental problems of production and large-scale organization, societies could ameliorate other problems, those of a social, moral, and psychological nature. What in fact occurred, on the testimony of a great deal of the most notable thought and writing, was a heightening of such problems. It would appear that as humans satisfy, relatively at least, the lower-order needs of food and shelter, their higher-order needs for purpose and meaning in life become ever more imperious. In the 20th century the idea of progress, though it had certainly not disappeared, was rivalled by ideas of cyclical change and of degeneration of society. It is hard to miss the currency of ideas in modern times—status, community, purpose, moral integration, on the one hand, and alienation, anomie, disintegration, breakdown on the other—that reveal only too clearly the divided nature of the human spirit and the unease of the human mind.

MARXIST INFLUENCES

Although Marxism had relatively little direct impact on sociology as a discipline in the West, it had enormous influence on states of mind that were closely associated with it—and with all of the social sciences. This was especially true during the 1930s, the decade of the Great Depression. Socialism remains for many an evocative symbol and creed. Marx remains a formidable name among intellectuals and is still, without any question, a principal intellectual source of radical movements in politics. Such a position cannot help but influence the contexts of even the most abstract of the social sciences.

What Marx's ideas have suggested above all else in a positive way is the possibility of a society directed not by blind forces of competition and struggle among economic elements but instead by directed planning. This hope, this image, proved a dominant one in the 20th century even where the influence of Marx and of socialism was at best small and indirect.

FREUDIAN INFLUENCES

Sigmund Freud

In the general area of personality, mind, and character, the writings of Sigmund Freud had influence on 20th-century culture and thought scarcely less than Marx's. His basic theories of the role of the unconscious mind, of the lasting effects of infantile sexuality, and of the Oedipus complex extended far beyond the discipline of psychoanalysis and even the larger area of psychiatry to areas of several of the social sciences. Sociology and social psychology have been influenced by Freudian ideas in their studies of social interaction and motivation. From Freud came the fruitful perspective that sees social behaviour and attitudes as generated not merely by the external situation but also by internal emotional needs springing from childhood—needs for recognition, authority, self-expression. Whatever may be the place directly occupied by Freud's ideas in the social sciences today, his influence upon 20th-century thought and culture generally, not excluding sociology, was hardly less than Marx's.

SPECIALIZATION AND CROSS-DISCIPLINARY APPROACHES

A major development in sociology and the other social sciences of the 20th century was the vast increase in the number of social scientists involved, in the number of academic and other centres of teaching and research in the social sciences, and in their degree of both comprehensiveness and specialization.

In the 21st century specialization has been as notable a tendency in the social sciences as in the biological and physical sciences. This is reflected not only in varieties of research but also in course offerings in academic departments. Whereas not very many years ago, a couple of dozen advanced courses in a social science reflected the specialization and diversity of the discipline even in major universities with graduate schools, today a hundred such courses are found to be not enough.

Side by side with this strong trend toward specialization, however, is another, countering trend: that of cross-fertilization and interdisciplinary cooperation. Today, evidences are all around of cross-disciplinary work and of fusion within a single social science of elements drawn from other social sciences. Thus there are such vital areas of work as political sociology, economic anthropology, psychology of voting, and industrial sociology. Single concepts such as "structure," "function," "alienation," and "motivation" can be seen employed variously to useful effect in several social sciences. The techniques of one social science can be seen consciously incorporated into another or into several social sciences. If history has provided much in the way of perspective to sociology or anthropology, each of these two has provided perspective, and also whole techniques, such as statistics and survey, to history. In short, specialization is by no means without some degree at least of countertendencies such as fusion and synthesis.

Another outstanding characteristic of each of the social sciences in the 20th century was its professionalization. Without exception, the social sciences became bodies of not merely research and teaching but also practice, in the sense that this word has in medicine or engineering. The number of sociologists, political scientists, and demographers to be found in government, industry, and private practice rises constantly.

THEORETICAL MODES

Though there is a great deal less of that grand or comprehensive theory that was a hallmark of 19th-century social philosophy and social science, there are still those persons who are engrossed in search for master principles, for general and unified theory that will assimilate all the lesser and more specialized types of theory. But their efforts and results are not often regarded as successful by the vast majority of social scientists. Theory tends to be specific theory—related to one or other of the major divisions of research within each of the social sciences.

DEVELOPMENTALISM

Developmentalism is another overall influence upon the work of the social sciences. As noted above, an interest in social evolution was one of the major aspects of the social sciences throughout the 19th century in western Europe. In the early 20th century, however, this interest, in its larger and more visible manifestations, seemed to terminate. There was a widespread reaction against the idea of unilinear sequences of stages, deemed by the 19th-century social evolutionists to be universal for all humankind in all places. Criticism of social evolution in this broad sense was a marked element of all the social sciences. There were numerous demonstrations of the inadequacy of unilinear descriptions of change when it came to accounting for what actually happened, so far as records and other evidences suggested, in the different areas and cultures of the world.

Beginning in the late 1940s and the 1950s, however, there was a resurgence of developmental ideas in all the social sciences—particularly with respect to studies of the new nations and cultures that were coming into existence in considerable numbers. Studies of economic growth and of political and social development became more and more numerous. Although it would be erroneous to see these developmental studies as simple repetitions of those of the 19th-century social evolutionists, there were, nevertheless, common elements of thought, including the idea of stages of growth and of change conceived as continuous and cumulative and even as moving toward some more or less common end. At their best, these studies of growth and development in the new nations, by their counterposing of traditional and modern ways, told a good deal about specific mechanisms of change, the result of the impact of the West upon outlying parts of the world. But as more and more social scientists became aware, efforts to place these concrete mechanisms of change into larger, more systematic models of development all too commonly succumbed to the same faults of unilinearity and specious universalism that early-20th-century critics found in 19th-century social evolution.

SOCIAL-SYSTEMS APPROACH

Still another major tendency in all of the social sciences after World War II was the interest in "social systems." The behaviour of individuals and groups was seen as falling into multiple interdependencies, and these interdependencies were considered sufficiently unified to warrant use of the word "system." Although there were clear uses of biological models and concepts in social-systems work, it may be fair to say that the greatest single impetus to development of this area was widening interest after World War II in cybernetics—the study of human control functions and of the electrical and mechanical systems that could be devised to replace or reinforce them. Concepts drawn from mechanical and electrical engineering were rather widespread in the study of social systems.

In social-systems studies, the actions and reactions of individuals, or even of groups as large as nations, are seen as falling within certain definable, more or less universal patterns of equilibrium and disequilibrium. The interdependence of roles, norms, and functions is regarded as fundamental in all types of group behaviour, large and small. Each social system, as encountered in social-science studies, is a kind of "ideal type," not identical to any specific "real" condition but sufficiently universal in terms of its central elements to permit useful generalization.

STRUCTURALISM AND FUNCTIONALISM

Structuralism in the social sciences is closely related to the theory of the social system. Although there is nothing new about the root concepts of structuralism—they may be seen in one form or other throughout Western thought—there is no question but that in the 20th century this view of behaviour became a dominant one in many fields. At bottom it is a reaction against all tendencies to deal with human thought and behaviour atomistically—that is, in terms of simple, discrete units of either thought, perception, or overt behaviour. In sociology, the idea of structure refers to the repetitive patternings that are found in the study of social existence. The structuralist contends that no element can be examined or explained outside its context or the pattern or structure of which it is a part. Indeed, it is the patterns, not the elements, that are the only valid objects of study.

What is called functionalism is closely related to structuralism, with the term "structural-functional" a common one in sociology. Function refers to the way in which behaviour takes on significance, not as a discrete act but as the dynamic aspect of some structure. Biological analogies are common in theories of structure and function in sociology. Very common is the image of the biological organ, with its close interdependence to other organs (as the heart to the lung) and the interdependence of activities (as circulation to respiration).

INTERACTIONISM

Interaction is still another concept that had wide currency in the social sciences, particularly sociology, of the 20th century. Social interaction—or, as it is sometimes called, symbolic interaction—refers to the fact that the relationships among two or more groups or human beings are never one-sided, purely physical, or direct. Always there is reciprocal influence, a mutual sense of "otherness." And always the presence of the "other" has crucial effect in one's definition of not merely what is external but what is internal. One acquires one's individual sense of identity from interactions with others beginning in infancy. It is the initial sense of the other person—mother, for example—that in time gives the child its sense of self, a sense that requires continuous development through later interactions with others. From the point of view of interactionist theory, all one's perceptions of and reactions to the external world are mediated or influenced by prior ideas, valuations, and assessments. Always one is engaged in socialization or the modification of one's mind, role, and behaviour through contact with others.

CHAPTER TWO

WHAT IS SOCIOLOGY?

Having explored the larger topic of the social sciences, let us turn our attention to a deeper examination of sociology. Sociology studies human societies, their interactions, and the processes that preserve and change them. It does this by examining the dynamics of constitu-

Sociology studies social institutions, such as educational systems.

ent parts of societies such as institutions, communities, populations, and gender, racial, or age groups. Sociology also studies social status or stratification, social movements, and social change, as well as societal disorder in the form of crime, deviance, and revolution.

Social life overwhelmingly regulates the behaviour of humans, largely because humans lack the instincts that guide most animal behaviour. Humans therefore depend on social institutions and organizations to inform their decisions and actions. Given the important role organizations play in influencing human action, it is sociology's task to discover how organizations affect the behaviour of persons, how they are established, how organizations interact with one another, how they decay, and, ultimately, how they disappear. Among the most basic organizational structures are economic, religious, educational, and political institutions, as well as more specialized institutions such as the family, the community, the military, peer groups, clubs, and volunteer associations.

The broad nature of sociological inquiry causes it to overlap with the other social sciences. Sociology's distinguishing feature is its practice of drawing on a larger societal context to explain social phenomena. Sociology devotes most of its attention to the collective aspects of human behaviour because sociologists place greater emphasis on the ways external groups influence the behaviour of individuals. Some of the key concepts studied by sociologists are examined in the following sections.

SOCIETY AND SOCIAL STRUCTURE

Sociologists study the organization of society. A society is community life thought of as a system within which the individual lives. It can be large or small, encompassing large groups of people or small sub-groups.

A society is a community in which people live and interact within social structures.

Human beings in a society interact and live together in a distinctive, stable arrangement of institutions known as social structures.

Studies of social structure attempt to explain such matters as integration and trends in inequality. In the study of these phenomena, sociologists analyze organizations, social categories (such as age groups), or rates (such as of crime or birth). This approach, sometimes called formal sociology, does not refer directly to individual behaviour or interpersonal interaction. Therefore, the study of social structure is not considered a behavioral science; at this level, the analysis is too abstract. It is a step removed from the consideration of concrete human behaviour, even though social-structural phenomena result from

Social Movements

A social movement is a loosely organized but sustained campaign in support of a social goal, typically either the implementation or the prevention of a change in society's structure or values. Although they differ in size, they are all essentially collective.

All definitions of social movement reflect the notion that social movements are intrinsically related to social change. They do not encompass the activities of people as members of stable social groups with established, unquestioned structures, norms, and values. The behaviour of members of social movements reflects the faith that people collectively can bring about or prevent social change if they will dedicate themselves to the pursuit of a goal.

One of the defining characteristics of a social movement is that it is relatively long lasting; the activity of the membership is sustained over a period of weeks, months, or even years rather than flaring up for a few hours or a few days and then disappearing.

A commonly used but highly subjective distinction is that between "reform" and "revolutionary" movements. A reform movement advocates a change that will preserve the existing values but will provide improved means of implementing them. A revolutionary movement is regarded as advocating replacement of existing values.

The end products of social movements are too complex to be seen as successes or failures. Failure may come as a result of ruthless suppression of the movement or through widespread apathy. A movement may wither away because too few take it seriously and it does not develop enough power to force its program on society.

humans responding to each other and to their environments. Those who study social structure do, however, follow an empirical (observational) approach to research, methodology, and epistemology.

Social structure is sometimes defined simply as patterned social relations—those regular and repetitive aspects of the interactions between the members of a given social entity. Even on this descriptive level, the concept is highly abstract: it selects only certain elements from ongoing social activities. The larger the social entity considered, the more abstract the concept tends to be. For this reason, the social structure of a small group is generally more closely related to the daily activities of its individual members than is the social structure of a larger society. In the study of larger social groups, the problem of selection is acute: much depends on what is included as components of the social structure.

In any society, social life is structured along the dimensions of time and space. Specific social activities take place at specific times, and time is divided into periods that are connected with the rhythms of social life—the routines of the day, the month, and the year. Specific social activities are also organized at specific places; particular places, for instance, are designated for such activities as working, worshiping, eating, and sleeping. Territorial boundaries delineate these places and are defined by rules of property that determine the use and possession of scarce goods. Additionally, in any society there is a more or less regular division of labour. Yet another universal structural characteristic of human societies is the regulation of violence. All violence is a potentially disruptive force; at the same time, it is a means of coercion and coordination of activities. Human beings have formed political units, such as nations, within which the use of violence is strictly regulated and which, at the same time, are organized for the use of violence against outside groups.

Furthermore, in any society there are arrangements within the structure for sexual reproduction and the care and education of the young. These arrangements take the form partly of kinship and marriage relations. Finally, systems of symbolic communication, particularly language, structure the interactions between the members of any society.

Societies rely on family units, based on kinship and marriage relations.

STRUCTURE AND SOCIAL ORGANIZATION

In the most general way, social structure is identified by those features of a social entity (a society or a group within a society) that persist over time, are interrelated, and influence both the functioning of the entity as a whole and the activities of its individual members. The origin of contemporary sociological references to social structure can be traced to Émile Durkheim, who argued that the parts of society are interdependent and that this interdependence imposes structure on the behaviour of institutions and their members. In other words, Durkheim believed that individual human behaviour is shaped by external forces. Similarly, American anthropologist George P. Murdock, in his book *Social Structure* (1949), examined kinship systems in preliterate societies and used social structure as a taxonomic device for classifying, comparing, and correlating various aspects of kinship systems.

Several ideas are implicit in the notion of social structure. First, human beings form social relations that are not arbitrary and coincidental but exhibit some regularity and continuity. Second, social life is not chaotic and formless but is, in fact, differentiated into certain groups, positions, and institutions that are interdependent or functionally interrelated. Third, individual choices are shaped and circumscribed by the social environment because social groups, although constituted by the social activities of individuals, are not a direct result of the wishes and intentions of the individual members. The notion of social structure implies, in other words, that human beings are not completely free and autonomous in their choices and actions but are instead constrained by the social world they inhabit and the social relations they form with one another.

SOCIAL STATUS

Social status is the relative rank that an individual holds, with attendant rights, duties, and lifestyle, in a social hierarchy based upon honour or prestige. Status may be ascribed—that is, assigned to individuals at birth without reference to any innate abilities—or achieved, requiring special qualities and gained through competition and individual effort. Ascribed status is typically based on sex, age, race, family relationships, or birth, while achieved status may be based on education, occupation, marital status, accomplishments, or other factors.

The word "status" implies social stratification on a vertical scale. People may be said to occupy high positions when they are able to control, by order or by influence, other people's conduct; when they derive prestige from holding important offices; or when their conduct is esteemed by others. Relative status is a major factor in determining the way people behave toward each other.

One's status tends to vary with social context. For example, the positions of persons in their kin group help determine their position in the larger community. The Native American Hopi lineage, although unnamed, contains the mechanism for transmitting rights to land, houses, and ceremonial knowledge and is thus vital to personal status. Among the Tallensi of Ghana, a boy who has lost his father is head of a household and therefore counts as an elder; a middle-aged man living under his father's roof is formally a child. Status may be governed by occupational considerations; thus, in parts of sub-Saharan

Social status can be based on lineage or merit, depending on the society's rules.

Africa blacksmiths commonly form a separate group of low status. In the Hindu caste system, sweepers are at the bottom of the scale because they handle excrement.

In most Western urban-industrial societies, such attributes as a respected occupation, the possession and consumption of material goods, physical appearance and dress, and etiquette and manners have become more important than lineage in determining one's social status. Occupations in these societies tend to be graded along a continuum rather than in a rigid hierarchy.

Status is closely correlated with etiquette and morality and in many societies rises with the liberal use of wealth. Manipulation of the wealth-status system in such cases often demands great individual effort, aggression, and chicanery.

Status groups are aggregates of persons arranged in a hierarchical social system. Such groups differ from social classes in being based on considerations of honour and prestige, rather than on economic status or power. Social stratification by status is common in premodern societies. The members of a status group interact mainly within their own group and to a lesser degree with those of higher or lower status. In some

CASTES

In some traditional societies in South Asia, one's place in society is determined by one's caste, a strictly regulated social group into which one is born. The caste system is especially important among the Hindus of India, where the system dates to ancient times. The various castes are ranked in a social and ritual hierarchy, with each group commanding the respect of lower-status castes and in turn giving respect to higher-status castes. One is usually expected to marry someone from one's own caste.

Hindu society is divided into more than 2,000 castes, known as *jati*s. Within a village, all the members of the same

Continued on page 34

Continued from page 33

jati recognize strong ties with each other and a sense of mutual obligation. At least in theory, *jati*s provide people with a sense of having a secure and well-defined social and economic role.

Each *jati* is associated with one of the four great social classes known as *varna*s: Brahmans (priests), Kshatriyas (warriors), Vaishyas (traders), and Shudras (laborers). The top-ranking Brahmans have traditionally been priests, advisers, and intellectual leaders. They are considered to be of greater ritual purity than members of the other *varna*s, and so they alone are thought to be capable of performing certain vital religious tasks.

Next in rank are the Kshatriyas, traditionally the military, ruling, and landowning class. Like the Brahmans, they enjoy great social prestige. The Kshatriyas are considered to be the nobility, with the main duty of protecting the state's people.

Clearly ranked below the two top categories are the Vaishyas. The members of this group were traditionally the commoners. Their role lay in productive work in agriculture and in trading. In modern times, the Vaishya class has become a symbol of middle-class respectability and prestige and is chiefly associated with commerce.

The members of the lowest-ranked *varna*, the Shudras, are traditionally artisans and laborers. According to Hindu tradition, their duty is to serve the three higher-ranked classes. Within the Shudra *varna*, there is a wide range of status groups, with some considered to be purer and to have a more-correct way of living than others.

Below the Shudras is a fifth group, without a *varna* designation. This group includes people whose jobs and ways of life typically bring them into contact with "pollutants" such as bodily fluids, dirt, leather, or dung. People who kill animals for a living, such as fisherman, also belong to this category, as do people who eat beef.

societies, clans or lineages may be ranked generally as aristocrats and commoners or graded from a royal clan down to clans that are stigmatized for lowly occupation or slave origin. Perhaps the most striking manifestation of status groups is found in the caste system of India. In Hindu villages there are usually members of a number of small endogamous groups (subcastes) based on traditional occupations, arranged from Brahmans to Untouchables. Contact with a person of lower caste (such as eating or drinking from his hands, bodily contact) pollutes the member of a higher caste and necessitates ritual purification. The age-grade system of many traditional East African societies may also resemble a status group.

SOCIAL CHANGE

Sociology also studies social change, the alteration of mechanisms within the social structure, characterized by changes in cultural symbols, rules of behaviour, social organizations, or value systems. Various theoretical schools emphasize different aspects of change. Marxist theory suggests that changes in modes of production can lead to changes in class systems, which can prompt other new forms of change or incite class conflict. A different view is conflict theory, which operates on a broad base that includes all institutions. The focus is not only on the purely divisive aspects of conflict because conflict, while inevitable, also brings about changes that promote social integration. Taking yet another approach, structural-functional theory emphasizes the integrating forces in society that ultimately minimize instability.

Social change can evolve from a number of different sources, including contact with other societies (diffusion), changes in the ecosystem (which can cause the loss of natural resources or widespread disease), technological change (epitomized by the Industrial Revolution, which created a new social group, the urban proletariat), and population growth and other demographic variables. Social change is also spurred by ideological, economic, and political movements.

This universal human potential for social change has a biological basis. It is rooted in the flexibility and adaptability of the human species—the near absence of biologically fixed action patterns (instincts) on the one hand and the enormous capacity for learning, symbolizing, and creating on the other hand. The human constitution makes possible changes that are not biologically (that is to say, genetically) determined. Social change, in other words, is possible only by virtue of biological characteristics of the human species, but the nature of the actual changes cannot be reduced to these species traits.

Several ideas of social change have been developed in various cultures and historical periods. Three may be distinguished as the most basic: (1) the idea of decline or degeneration, (2) the idea of cyclic change, a pattern of subsequent and recurring phases of growth and decline, and (3) the idea of continuous progress.

Progress was the key idea in 19th-century theories of social evolution, and evolutionism was the common core shared by the most influential social theories of that century. Evolutionism implied that humans progressed along one line of development, that this development was predetermined and inevitable, since it corresponded to definite laws, that some societies were more advanced in this development than were others, and that Western society was the most advanced of these and therefore indicated the future of the rest of the world's population. This line of thought has since been disputed and disproved.

Following a different approach, Auguste Comte advanced a "law of three stages," according to which human societies progress from a theological stage, which is dominated by religion, through a metaphysical stage, in which abstract speculative thinking is most prominent, and onward toward a positivist stage, in which empirically based scientific theories prevail.

The most encompassing theory of social evolution was developed by Herbert Spencer, who, unlike Comte, linked social evolution to biological evolution. According to Spencer, biological organisms and human societies follow the same universal, natural evolutionary law: "a change from a state of relatively indefinite, incoherent, homogeneity to a state of relatively definite, coherent, heterogeneity." In other words, as societies grow in size, they become more complex; their parts differentiate, specialize into different functions, and become, consequently, more interdependent.

The work of Durkheim, Weber, and other social theorists around the turn of the 20th century marked a transition from evolutionism toward more static theories. Evolutionary theories were criticized on empirical grounds—they could be refuted by a growing mass of research findings—and because of their determinism and Western-centred optimism. Theories of cyclic change that denied long-term progress gained popularity in the first half of the 20th century.

The study of long-term social change revived in the 1950s and continued to develop through the 1960s and '70s. Neoevolutionist theories were proclaimed by several anthropologists who held to the idea of social evolution as a long-term development that is both patterned and cumulative. Unlike 19th-century evolutionism, neoevolutionism does not assume that all societies go through the same stages of development. Instead, much attention is paid to variations between societies as well as to relations of influence among them. The latter concept has come to be known by the term "acculturation." In addition, social evolution is not regarded as predetermined or inevitable but is understood in terms of probabilities. Finally, evolutionary development is not equated with progress.

Theories of social change, both old and new, commonly assume that the course of social change is not arbitrary but is, to a certain degree, regular or patterned. The three traditional ideas of social change—decline, cyclic change, and progress—have unquestionably influenced modern theories. Yet because these theories are not scientifically determined, they fail to make an explicit distinction between decline and progress. In fact, the qualities of decline and progress cannot be derived scientifically (that is, from empirical observations) alone but are instead identified by normative evaluations and value judgments. If the study of social change is to be conducted on scientific and nonnormative terms, then, only two basic patterns of social change can be considered: the cyclic, as identified above, and the one-directional. Often the time span of the change determines which pattern is observed.

EXPLANATIONS OF SOCIAL CHANGE

One way of explaining social change is to show causal connections between two or more processes. This may take the form of determinism or reductionism, both of which tend to explain social change by reducing it to one supposed autonomous and all-determining causal process. A more cautious assumption is that one process has relative causal priority, without implying that this process is completely autonomous and all-determining. What follows are some of the processes thought to contribute to social change.

Changes in the natural environment may result from climatic variations, natural disasters, or the spread of disease. For example, both worsening of climatic conditions and the Black Death epidemics are thought to have contributed to the crisis of feudalism in 14th-century Europe. Changes in the natural environment may be either independent of human social activities or caused by them. Deforestation, erosion, and air pollution belong to the latter category, and they in turn may have far-reaching social consequences.

Population growth and increasing population density represent demographic forms of social change. Population growth may lead to geographic expansion of a society, military conflicts, and the intermingling of cultures. Increasing population density may stimulate technological innovations, which in turn may increase the division of labour, social differentiation, commercialization, and urbanization. This sort of process occurred in western Europe from the 11th to the 13th century and in England in the 18th century, where population growth spurred the Industrial Revolution. On the other hand, population growth may contribute to economic stagnation and increasing poverty, as may be witnessed in several developing countries today.

Several theories of social evolution identify technological innovations as the most important determinants of societal change. Such technological breakthroughs as the smelting of iron, the introduction of the plow in agriculture, the invention of the steam engine, and the development of the computer have had lasting social consequences.

Technological changes are often considered in conjunction with economic processes. These include the formation and extension of markets, modifications of property relations (such as the change from feudal lord-peasant relations to contractual proprietor-tenant relations), and changes in the organization of labour (such as the change from independent craftsmen to factories). Historical materialism, as developed by Marx and Engels, is one of the more prominent theories that gives priority to economic processes, but it is not the only one. Indeed, materialist theories have even been developed in opposition to Marxism. One of these theories, the "logic of industrialization" thesis by American scholar Clark Kerr and his colleagues, states that industrialization everywhere has similar consequences, whether the property relations are called capitalist or communist.

Other theories have stressed the significance of ideas as causes of social change. Comte's law of three stages is such a theory. Weber regarded religious ideas as important contributors to economic development or stagnation; according to his controversial thesis, the individualistic ethic of Christianity, and in particular Calvinism, partially explains the rise of the capitalist spirit, which led to economic dynamism in the West.

A change in collective ideas is not merely an intellectual process; it is often connected to the formation of new social movements. This in itself might be regarded as a potential cause of social change. Weber called attention to this factor in conjunction with his concept of "charismatic leadership." The charismatic leader, by virtue of the extraordinary personal qualities attributed to him, is able to create a group of followers who are willing to break established rules. Examples include Jesus, Napoleon, and Hitler. Recently, however, the concept of charisma has been trivialized to refer to almost any popular figure.

Changes in the regulation of violence, in the organization of the state, and in international relations may also contribute to social change. For example, German sociologist Norbert Elias interpreted the formation of states in western Europe as a relatively autonomous process that led to increasing control of violence and, ultimately, to rising standards of self-control. According to other theories of political revolution, such as those proposed by American historical sociologist Charles Tilly, the functioning of the state apparatus itself and the nature of interstate relations are of decisive importance in the outbreak of a revolution: it is only when the state is not able to fulfill its basic functions of maintaining law

Technology and social media were key to social change during the Arab Spring.

and order and defending territorial integrity that revolutionary groups have any chance of success.

The causes of social change are diverse, and the processes of change can be identified as either short-term trends or long-term developments. Change can be either cyclic or one-directional. The mechanisms of social change can be varied and interconnected. Several mechanisms may be combined in one explanatory model of social change. For example, innovation by business might be stimulated by competition and by government regulation.

To the degree that processes of change are regular and interconnected, social change itself is structured. Since about 1965 there has been a shift in emphasis from "structure" to "change" in social theory. Change on different levels—social dynamics in everyday life and short-term transformations and long-term developments in society at large—has become the focus of much attention in the study of society.

CHAPTER THREE

THE ORIGINS OF SOCIOLOGY

The founders of sociology spent decades searching for the proper direction of the new discipline. They tried several highly divergent pathways, some driven by methods and contents borrowed from other sciences, others invented by the scholars themselves. To better view the various turns the discipline has taken, the development of sociology may be divided into four periods: the establishment of the discipline from the late 19th century until World War I, interwar consolidation, explosive growth from 1945 to 1975, and the subsequent period of segmentation.

Though sociology draws on the Western tradition of rational inquiry established by the ancient Greeks, it is specifically the offspring of 18th- and 19th-century philosophy and has been viewed, along with economics and political science, as a reaction against speculative philosophy and folklore. Consequently, sociology separated from moral philosophy to become a specialized discipline. While he is not credited with the founding of the discipline of sociology, French philosopher Auguste Comte is recognized for having coined the term "sociology."

AUGUSTE COMTE

Auguste Comte (1798–1857) lived through the aftermath of the French Revolutionary and Napoleonic periods, at a time when a new, stable social order—without despotism—was sought. Modern science and technology and the Industrial Revolution had begun transforming the societies of Europe in directions no one yet understood. People experienced violent

An armed mob of Parisians storm the Bastille on July 14, 1789, at the start of the French Revolution.

conflict but were adrift in feeling, thought, and action; they lacked confidence in established sentiments, beliefs, and institutions but had nothing with which to replace them. Comte thought that this condition was not only significant for France and Europe but was one of the decisive junctures of human history.

Comte's particular ability was as a synthesizer of the most diverse intellectual currents. He took his ideas mainly from writers of the 18th and early 19th centuries. From David Hume and Immanuel Kant he derived his conception of positivism—*i.e.,* the theory that theology and metaphysics are earlier imperfect modes of knowledge and that positive knowledge is based on natural phenomena and their properties and relations as verified by the empirical sciences. From various French clericalist thinkers Comte took the notion of a hypothetical framework for social organization that would imitate the hierarchy and discipline found in the Roman Catholic church. From various Enlightenment philosophers he adopted the notion of historical progress. Most importantly, from Henri de Saint-Simon, a French social reformer and one of the founders of socialism, he came to appreciate the need for a basic and unifying social science that would both explain existing social organizations and guide social planning for a better future. This new science he called "sociology" for the first time.

Comte believed that social phenomena could be reduced to laws in the same way that the revolutions of the heavenly bodies had been made explicable by gravitational theory. Furthermore, he believed that the purpose of the new scientific analysis of society should be ameliorative and that the ultimate outcome of all innovation and systematization in the new science should be the guidance of social planning. Comte also thought a new and secularized spiritual order was needed to supplant what he viewed as the outdated supernaturalism of Christian theology.

Comte's main contribution to positivist philosophy falls into five parts: his rigorous adoption of the scientific method; his law of the three states or stages of intellectual development; his classification of the sciences; his conception of the incomplete philosophy of each of these sciences anterior to sociology; and his synthesis of a positivist social philosophy in a unified form. He sought a system of philosophy that could form a basis for political organization appropriate to modern industrial society.

Comte's "law of the three stages" maintained that human intellectual development had moved historically from a theological stage, in which the world and human destiny within it were explained in terms of gods and spirits; through a transitional metaphysical stage, in which explanations were in terms of essences, final causes, and other abstractions; and finally to the modern positive stage. This last stage was distinguished by an awareness of the limitations of human knowledge. Knowledge could only be relative to human nature and to humans' varying social and historical situations. Absolute explanations were therefore better abandoned for the more sensible discovery of laws based on the observable relations between phenomena.

Though Comte did not originate the concept of sociology or its area of study, he greatly extended and elaborated the field and systematized its content. Comte divided sociology into two main fields, or branches: social statics, or the study of the forces that hold society together; and social dynamics, or the study of the causes of social change. He held that the underlying principles of society are individual egoism, which is encouraged by the division of labour, and the combination of efforts and the maintenance of social cohesion by means of government and the state.

Comte revealed his conception of the ideal positivist society in his *System of Positive Polity*. He believed that the organization of the Roman Catholic church, divorced from Christian theology, could provide a structural and symbolic model for the new society, though Comte substituted a "religion of humanity" for the worship of God. A spiritual priesthood of secular sociologists would guide society and control education and public morality. The actual administration of the government and of the economy would be in the hands of businessmen and bankers, while the maintenance of private morality would be the province of women as wives and mothers.

Harriet Martineau

She is not widely studied in sociology classes today, but Harriet Martineau (1802–1876) was one of the founders of the discipline. Perhaps her most scholarly work is *The Positive Philosophy of Auguste Comte, Freely Translated and Condensed*, 2 vol. (1853), her version of Comte's *Cours de philosophie positive*.

Continued on page 46

Continued from page 45

Martineau first gained a large reading public with a series of stories popularizing classical economics, especially the ideas of Thomas Robert Malthus and David Ricardo: *Illustrations of Political Economy*, 25 vol. (1832–34), *Poor Laws and Paupers Illustrated*, 10 vol. (1833–34), and *Illustrations of Taxation*, 5 vol. (1834). After a visit to the United States (1834–36), concerning which she wrote the incisively sociological *Society in America* (1837) and the more anecdotal *Retrospect of Western Travel* (1838), she espoused the then unpopular abolition movement. Her best-known novels, including *Deerbrook* (1839) and *The Hour and the Man* (1841), were also written during this period. She helped to found the popular genre of the school story with *The Crofton Boys* (1841) and pioneered "back to the land" journalism with her writings about her garden in England's Lake District.

A trip to the Middle East in 1846 led Martineau to study the evolution of religions. She became increasingly skeptical of religious beliefs, including her own liberal Unitarianism, and her avowal of atheism in the *Letters on the Laws of Man's Nature and Development* (1851, with H.G. Atkinson) caused widespread shock. Her chief historical work, *The History of the Thirty Years' Peace, A.D. 1816–1846* (1849), was a widely read popular treatment. She also contributed voluminously to periodicals, writing some 1,600 leading articles for the *Daily News* between 1852 and 1866. Her *Biographical Sketches* (1869, enlarged 1877) was a collection of articles written for the *Daily News* on various well-known contemporaries, including Charlotte Brontë. Martineau lost her hearing early in life and later had heart disease and other illnesses. Her candid *Autobiography*, edited by Maria Weston Chapman, was published posthumously (3 vol., 1877).

Though unquestionably a man of genius, Comte inspired discipleship on the one hand and derision on the other. His plans for a future society have been described as ludicrous, and Comte was deeply reactionary in his rejection of democracy, his emphasis on hierarchy and obedience, and his opinion that the ideal government would be made up of an intellectual elite. But his ideas influenced such notable social scientists as Émile Durkheim of France and Herbert Spencer and Sir Edward Burnett Tylor of Great Britain. Comte's belief in the importance of sociology as the scientific study of human society remains an article of faith among contemporary sociologists, and the work he accomplished remains a remarkable synthesis and an important system of thought.

FOUNDING THE DISCIPLINE

Some of the earliest sociologists developed an approach based on Darwinian evolutionary theory. In their attempts to establish a scientifically based academic discipline, a line of creative thinkers, including Herbert Spencer, Benjamin Kidd, Lewis H. Morgan, E.B. Tylor, and L.T. Hobhouse, developed analogies between human society and the biological organism. They introduced into sociological theory such biological concepts as variance, natural selection, and inheritance—asserting that these evolutionary factors resulted in the progress of societies from stages of savagery and barbarism to civilization by virtue of the survival of the fittest. Some writers believed that these stages of society could be seen in the developmental stages of each individual. Strange customs were explained by assuming that they were throwbacks to useful practices of an earlier period, such as the make-believe struggle sometimes enacted between the bridegroom and the bride's relatives reflecting the earlier custom of bride capture. In its popular period of the late 19th and early 20th centuries, social Darwinism, along with the doctrines of Adam Smith and Thomas Malthus, touted unrestricted competition and laissez-faire so that the "fittest" would survive and civilization

Charles Darwin

would continue to advance. Although the popularity of social Darwinism waned in the 20th century, the ideas on competition and analogies from biological ecology were appropriated by the Chicago School of sociology (a University of Chicago program focusing on urban studies, founded by Albion Small in 1892) to form the theory of human ecology that endures as a viable study approach.

HERBERT SPENCER

Herbert Spencer advocated the preeminence of the individual over society and of science over religion. He was one of the most argumentative and most discussed English thinkers of the Victorian period. His strongly scientific orientation led him to urge the importance of examining social phenomena in a scientific way. He believed that all aspects of his thought formed a coherent and closely ordered system. Science and philosophy, he held, gave support to and enhanced individualism and progress. Though it is natural to cite him as the great exponent of Victorian optimism, it is notable that he was by no means unaffected by the pessimism that from time to time clouded the Victorian confidence. Evolution, he taught, would be followed by dissolution, and individualism would come into its own only after an era of socialism and war.

Spencer saw philosophy as a synthesis of the fundamental principles of the special sciences, a sort of scientific summa to replace the theological systems of the Middle Ages. He thought of unification in terms of development, and his whole scheme was in fact suggested to him by the evolution of biological species. In *First Principles* he argued that there is a fundamental law of matter, which he called the law of the persistence of force, from which it follows that nothing homogeneous can remain as such if it is acted upon, because any external force must affect some part of it differently from other parts and cause difference and variety to arise. From this, he continued, it would follow that any force that continues to act on what is homogeneous must bring about an increasing variety. This "law of the multiplication of effects," due to an unknown and unknowable absolute force, is in Spencer's view the clue to the understanding of all development, cosmic as well as biological. It should be noted that Spencer published his idea of the evolution of biological species before the views of Charles Darwin and the British naturalist Alfred Russel Wallace were known, but Spencer at that time thought that evolution was caused by the inheritance of acquired characteristics, whereas Darwin and Wallace attributed it to natural selection. Spencer later accepted the theory that natural selection was one of the causes of biological evolution, and he himself coined the phrase "survival of the fittest" (*Principles of Biology* [1864], vol. 1, p. 444).

That Spencer first derived his general evolutionary scheme from reflection on human society is seen in *Social Statics,* in which social evolution is held to be a process of increasing "individuation." He saw human societies as evolving by means of increasing division of labour from undifferentiated hordes into complex civilizations. Spencer believed that the fundamental sociological classification was between military societies, in which cooperation was secured by force, and industrial societies, in which cooperation was voluntary and spontaneous.

Evolution is not the only biological conception that Spencer applied in his sociological theories. He made a detailed comparison between animal organisms and human societies. In both he found a regulative system (the central nervous system in the one, government in the other), a sustaining system (alimentation in the one case, industry in the other), and a distribution system (veins and arteries in the first; roads, telegraphs, etc., in the second). The great difference between an animal and a social organism, he said, is that, whereas in the former there is one consciousness relating to the whole, in the latter consciousness exists in each member only; society exists for the benefit of its members and not they for its benefit.

This individualism is the key to all of Spencer's work. His contrast between military and industrial societies is drawn between despotism, which is primitive and bad, and individualism, which is civilized and good. He believed that in industrial society the order achieved, though planned by no one, is delicately adjusted to the needs of all parties.

Spencer's attempt to synthesize the sciences showed a sublime audacity that has not been repeated because the intellectual specialization he welcomed and predicted increased even beyond his expectations. His sociology, although it gave an impetus to the study of society, was superseded as a result of the development of social anthropology since his day and was much more concerned with providing a rationale for his social ideals than he himself appreciated. So-called "primitive" (tribal and indigenous) peoples, for example, are not the childlike emotional creatures that he thought them to be, nor is religion to be explained only in terms of the souls of ancestors.

E.B. TYLOR

Sir Edward Burnett Tylor (1832–1917) was an English anthropologist regarded as the founder of cultural anthropology. His most important work, *Primitive Culture* (1871), influenced in part by Darwin's theory of biological evolution, developed the theory of an evolutionary, progressive relationship from primitive to modern cultures. He is best known

INDIVIDUALISM

Individualism is a political and social philosophy that emphasizes the moral worth of the individual. Although the concept of an individual may seem straightforward, there are many ways of understanding it, both in theory and in practice.

In the United States, individualism became part of the core American ideology by the 19th century, incorporating the influences of New England Puritanism, Jeffersonianism, and the philosophy of natural rights. "Rugged individualism"—extolled by Herbert Hoover during his presidential campaign in 1928—was associated with traditional American values such as personal freedom, capitalism, and limited government.

Other aspects of individualism pertain to a series of different questions about how to conceive the relation between collectivities and individuals. One such question focuses on how facts about the behaviour of groups, about social processes, and about large-scale historical events are to be explained. Another question that arises in debates over individualism is how objects of worth or value (i.e., goods) in moral and political life are to be conceived. Some theorists, known as atomists, argue that no such goods are intrinsically common or communal, maintaining instead that there are only individual goods that accrue to individuals. According to this perspective, morality and politics are merely the instruments through which each individual attempts to secure such goods for himself.

Individualism, with its endorsement of private enjoyments and control of one's personal environment and its neglect of public involvement and communal attachment, has long been lamented and criticized from both the right and the left and from both religious and secular perspectives. Especially notable

Continued on page 52

Continued on page 51

critiques have been made by advocates of communitarianism, who tend to equate individualism with narcissism and selfishness. Likewise, thinkers in the tradition of "republican" political thought—according to which power is best controlled by being divided—are disturbed by their perception that individualism deprives the state of the support and active involvement of citizens, thereby impairing democratic institutions. Individualism also has been thought to distinguish modern Western societies from premodern and non-Western ones, such as traditional India and China, where, it is said, the community or the nation is valued above the individual and an individual's role in the political and economic life of his community is largely determined by his membership in a specific class or caste.

today for providing, in this book, one of the earliest and clearest definitions of culture, one that is widely accepted and used by contemporary anthropologists. Culture, he said, is "that complex whole which includes knowledge, belief, art, morals, law, custom, and any other capabilities and habits acquired by man as a member of society."

Tylor published three major works. *Researches into the Early History of Mankind and the Development of Civilization* (1865), which immediately established his reputation as a leading anthropologist, elaborated the thesis that cultures past and present, civilized and primitive, must be studied as parts of a single history of human thought. "The past," he wrote, "is continually needed to explain the present, and the whole to explain the part." Tylor's fame, however, is based chiefly upon the publication of *Primitive Culture.* In it he again traced a progressive development from a savage to a civilized state and pictured primitive man as an early philosopher applying his reason to explain events in the human and natural world that were beyond his control, even though his scientific ignorance produced erroneous explanations. Tylor identified, for example, the earliest form of religious belief as "animism," a belief in spiritual beings, arrived at, he assumed, by primitive attempts to explain the difference between the living body and the corpse and the separation of soul and body in dreams. Primitive Culture also elaborated upon a theme that became a central concept in his work: the relation of primitive cultures to modern populations

> By long experience of the course of human society, the principle of development in culture has become so ingrained in our philosophy that ethnologists, of whatever school, hardly doubt but that, whether by progress or degradation, savagery and civilization are connected as lower and higher stages of one formation.

Thus, "culture" should be studied not only in the artistic and spiritual achievements of civilizations but in man's technological and moral accomplishments made at all stages of his development. Tylor noted how customs and beliefs from a distant, primitive past seemed to have lived on into the modern world, and he became well-known for his examination of such "survivals," a concept that he introduced. His evolutionary view of human development was endorsed by most of his colleagues and, of course, by Charles Darwin, who had established biological evolution as the key to the emergence of the human species.

In the late 19th-century political and theological controversy over the question whether all the races of mankind belonged physically and mentally to a single species, Tylor was a powerful advocate of the physical and psychological unity of all mankind. On this question, as in all anthropological disputes, he based his position on respect for empirical evidence, which he hoped would bring the standards and procedures of the natural sciences to the study of humanity.

His last book, *Anthropology, an Introduction to the Study of Man and Civilization* (1881), is an excellent summary of what was, late in the 19th century, known and thought in that field. Like all Tylor's work, it conveys a vast quantity of information in a lucid and energetic style.

Tylor was made a fellow of the Royal Society in 1871 and given a doctorate of civil law at the University of Oxford in 1875. Eight years later he returned to Oxford to give lectures and stayed there as keeper of the university's museum, becoming reader in anthropology in 1884 and the first professor of anthropology in 1896. He was also elected the first Gifford lecturer at Aberdeen University in 1888. He retired from active life in 1909 and died in 1917.

LEWIS HENRY MORGAN

The American Lewis Henry Morgan's kinship studies on Native Americans led him to develop his theory of cultural evolution, which was set forth in *Ancient Society, or Researches in the Lines of Human Progress from Savagery through Barbarism to Civilization* (1877). This was among the first major scientific accounts of the origin and evolution of civilization. Morgan posited that advances in social organization arose primarily from changes in food production. Society had progressed from a hunting-and-gathering stage (which he denoted by the term "savagery") to a stage of settled agriculture ("barbarism") and then on to an urban society possessing a more advanced agriculture ("civilization"). He illustrated these developmental stages with examples drawn from various cultures. Morgan's ideas about the development of technology over time have come to be regarded as generally correct in their fundamental aspects. His theory that human social life advanced from an initial stage of promiscuity through various forms of family life that culminated in monogamy has long been held obsolete, however.

Morgan's emphasis on the importance of technological change and other purely material factors in cultural and social evolution attracted the attention of Karl Marx and Friedrich Engels. That *Ancient Society* came to be regarded by Marxists as a classic was largely the result of the importance that Marx and Engels attached to it because Morgan's own social allegiance was to the industrial and commercial middle class and its achievements.

Lewis Henry Morgan

LEONARD HOBHOUSE

The English sociologist Leonard Trelawny Hobhouse tried to reconcile liberalism with collectivism in the interest of social progress. In elaborating his conception of sociology, he drew on his knowledge of several other fields: philosophy, psychology, biology, anthropology, and the history of religion, ethics, and law. Interested in the process of social change, Hobhouse tried to correlate such change with its contribution to the general advance of the community; he also studied the history of knowledge, morals, and religions in relation to social change.

Questioning the social theories most frequently advocated in England in his time, Hobhouse rejected the idea of laissez-faire because he believed that a certain degree of universal cooperation is necessary to the fulfillment of the potentialities of individuals. At the same time, he disapproved of Fabian socialism because it fostered a kind of cooperation that might, in his view, lead to a mere bureaucracy, hindering progress.

Among Hobhouse's works are *The Theory of Knowledge* (1896), *Development and Purpose* (1913), intended as a full statement of his philosophy, and four books collectively entitled *The Principles of Sociology.* They are *The Metaphysical Theory of the State* (1918), *The Rational Good* (1921), *The Elements of Social Justice* (1922), and *Social Development* (1924).

SOCIAL DARWINISM

Social Darwinism is the theory that persons, groups, and races are subject to the same laws of natural selection as Charles Darwin had perceived in plants and animals in nature. According to the theory, which was popular in the late 19th and early 20th centuries, the weak were diminished and their cultures delimited, while the strong grew in power and in cultural influence over the weak. Social Darwinists held that the life of humans in society was a struggle for existence ruled by "survival of the fittest," a phrase proposed by the British philosopher and scientist Herbert Spencer.

The social Darwinists—notably Spencer and Walter Bagehot in England and William Graham Sumner in the United States—believed that the process of natural selection acting on variations in the population would result in the survival of the best competitors and in continuing improvement in the population. Societies, like individuals, were viewed as organisms that evolve in this manner.

William Graham Sumner

The theory was used to support laissez-faire capitalism and political conservatism. Class stratification was justified on the basis of "natural" inequalities among individuals, for the control of property was said to be a correlate of superior and inherent moral attributes such as industriousness, temperance, and frugality. Attempts to reform society through state intervention or other means would, therefore, interfere with natural processes; unrestricted competition and defense of the status quo were in accord with biological selection. The poor were the "unfit" and should not be aided; in the struggle for existence, wealth was a sign of success. At the societal level, social Darwinism was used as a philosophical rationalization for imperialist, colonialist, and racist policies, sustaining belief in Anglo-Saxon or Aryan cultural and biological superiority.

Social Darwinism declined during the 20th century as an expanded knowledge of biological, social, and cultural phenomena undermined, rather than supported, its basic tenets.

CHAPTER FOUR

EARLY SOCIOLOGICAL THEORIES

Since the initial interest in evolutionary theory, sociologists have considered four deterministic theories to replace social Darwinism. This search for new approaches began prior to World War I as emphasis shifted from economic theory to geographic, psychological, and cultural theory—roughly in that order.

ECONOMIC DETERMINISM

The first of the deterministic theories, economic determinism, reflects the interest many sociologists had in the thought of Karl Marx. In Marx's view, the dialectical nature of history is expressed in class struggle. With the development of capitalism, the class struggle takes an acute form. Two basic classes, around which other less important classes are grouped, oppose each other in the capitalist system: the owners of the means of production, or bourgeoisie, and the workers, or proletariat. As he wrote in "The Communist Manifesto," because "the bourgeois relations of production are the last contradictory form of the process of social production, contradictory not in the sense of an individual contradiction, but of a contradiction that is born of the conditions of social existence of individuals; however, the forces of production which develop in the midst of bourgeois society create at the same time the material conditions for resolving this contradiction. With this social development the prehistory of human society ends."

When people have become aware of their loss, of their alienation, as a universal nonhuman situation, it will be possible for them to proceed to a radical transformation of their situation by a revolution. This revolution will be the prelude to the establishment of communism and the reign of liberty reconquered. "In the place of the old bourgeois society with its classes and its class antagonisms, there will be an association in which the free development of each is the condition for the free development of all."

But for Marx there are two views of revolution. One is that of a final conflagration, "a violent suppression of the old conditions of production," which occurs when the opposition between bourgeoisie and proletariat has been carried to its extreme point. This conception is set forth in a manner inspired by the Hegelian dialectic of the master and the slave, in "Die heilige Familie" (1845; "The Holy Family"). The other conception is that of a permanent revolution involving a provisional coalition between the proletariat and the petty bourgeoisie rebelling against a capitalism that is only superficially united. Once a majority has been won to the coalition, an unofficial proletarian authority constitutes itself alongside the revolutionary bourgeois authority. Its mission is the political and revolutionary education of the proletariat, gradually assuring the transfer of legal power from the revolutionary bourgeoisie to the revolutionary proletariat.

If one reads "The Communist Manifesto" carefully one discovers inconsistencies that indicate that Marx had not reconciled the concepts of catastrophic and of permanent revolution. Moreover, Marx never analyzed classes as specific groups of people opposing other groups of people. Depending on the writings and the periods, the number of classes varies; and unfortunately the pen fell from Marx's hand at the moment when, in "Das Kapital" (vol. 3), he was about to take up the question. Reading "Das Kapital," one is furthermore left with an ambiguous impression with regard to the destruction of capitalism: will it be the result of the "general crisis" that Marx expects, or of the action of the conscious proletariat, or of both at once?

Economic determinism reflects many of Marx's ideas, such as the idea that social differentiation and class conflict resulted from economic factors. This approach had its greatest popularity in Europe, where it remained a strong influence on some sociologists until the 1980s. It did not gain a significant foothold in the United States because American society was thought to be socially mobile, classless, and oriented to the individual. This neglect of Marxism by American sociologists, however, was not due to scholarly ignorance. Sociologists of all periods had read Marx as well as Charles A. Beard's economic interpretation of American history and the work of Werner Sombart (who had been a Marxist in his early career). Instead, in the 1960s, neo-Marxism—an amalgam of theories of stratification by Marx and Max Weber—gained strong support among a minority of sociologists. Their enthusiasm lasted about 30 years, ebbing with the breakup of the Soviet system and the introduction of postindustrial doctrines that linked class systems to a bygone industrial era. The persistence of social and economic inequality is now explained as a complex outcome of factors, including gender, race, and region, as well as global trade and national politics.

HUMAN ECOLOGY

Representing the second theoretical area, human geographers—Ellsworth Huntington, Ellen Semple, Friedrich Ratzel, Paul Vidal de La Blache, Jean Brunhes, and others—emphasized the impact of climate and geography on the evolution of those societies that flourished in temperate zones. Their theories found no place in mainstream sociological thought, however, except for a brief period in the 1930s when human ecology sought to explain social change by linking environmental conditions with demographic, organizational, and technological factors. Human ecology remains a small but vital part of sociology today.

Human ecology is a theory suggesting man's collective interaction with his environment. Influenced by the work of biologists on the

Max Weber

interaction of organisms within their environments, social scientists undertook to study human groups in a similar way. Thus, ecology in the social sciences is the study of the ways in which the social structure adapts to the quality of natural resources and to the existence of other human groups. When this study is limited to the development and variation of cultural properties, it is called cultural ecology.

Human ecology views the biological, environmental, demographic, and technical conditions of the life of any people as an interrelated series of determinants of form and function in human cultures and social systems. It recognizes that group behaviour is dependent upon resources and associated skills and upon a body of emotionally charged beliefs; these together give rise to a system of social structures.

SOCIAL PSYCHOLOGY

Psychological theories emphasized instincts, drives, motives, temperament, intelligence, and human sociability in social behaviour and societal evolution. Social psychology modifies these concepts to explain the broader phenomena of social interaction or small group behaviour. Although American sociology even today retains an individualistic bias, by the 1930s sociologists had concluded that psychological factors alone could not explain the behaviour of larger groups and societies.

Social psychology is the scientific study of the behaviour of individuals in their social and cultural setting. Although the term may be taken to include the social activity of laboratory animals or those in the wild, the emphasis here is on human social behaviour. Once a relatively speculative, intuitive enterprise, social psychology has become an active form of empirical investigation, the volume of research literature having risen rapidly after about 1925. Social psychologists now have a substantial volume of observation data covering a range of topics; the evidence remains loosely coordinated, however, and the field is beset by many different theories and conceptual schemes.

Early impetus in research came from the United States, and much work in other countries has followed U.S. tradition, though independent research efforts are being made elsewhere in the world. Social psychology is being actively pursued in the United Kingdom, Canada, Australia, Germany, the Netherlands, France, Belgium, Scandinavia, Japan, and Russia. Most social psychologists are members of university departments of psychology; others are in departments of sociology or work in such applied settings as industry and government.

Much research in social psychology has consisted of laboratory experiments on social behaviour, but this approach has been criticized in recent years as being too stultifying, artificial, and unrealistic. Much of the conceptual background of research in social psychology derives from other fields of psychology. While learning theory and psychoanalysis were once most influential, cognitive and linguistic approaches to research have become more popular; sociological contributions also have been influential.

Social psychologists are employed, or used as consultants, in setting up the social organization of businesses and psychiatric communities; some work to reduce conflict between ethnic groups, to design mass communications (e.g., advertising), and to advise on child rearing. They have helped in the treatment of mental patients and in the rehabilitation of convicts. Fundamental research in social psychology has been brought to the attention of the public through popular books and in the periodical press.

In some laboratory experiments, subjects watch stills or moving pictures, listen to audio recordings, or directly observe or interact with another person. Subjects may be asked to reveal their social perception of such persons on rating scales, to give free descriptions of them, or to respond evaluatively in other ways. Although such studies can produce results that do not correspond to those in real-life settings, they can provide useful information on the perception of personality, social roles, emotions, and interpersonal attitudes or responses during ongoing social interaction.

Research has been directed to how social perception is affected by cultural stereotypes (e.g., racial prejudice), by inferences from different verbal and nonverbal cues, by the pattern of perceptual activity during social interaction, and by the general personality structure of the perceiver. The work has found practical application in the assessment of employees and of candidates for positions.

There also has been research on the ways in which perception of objects and people is affected by social factors such as culture and group membership. It has been shown, for example, how coins, colours, and other physical cues are categorized differently by people as a result of their group membership and of the categories provided by language. Other studies have shown the effect of group pressures on perception.

The different verbal and nonverbal signals used in conversation have been studied, and the functions of such factors as gaze, gesture, and tone of voice are analyzed in social-interaction studies. Social interaction is thus seen to consist of closely related sequences of nonverbal signals and verbal utterances. Gaze has been found to perform several important functions. Laboratory and field studies have examined helping behaviour, imitation, friendship formation, and social interaction in psychotherapy.

Among the theoretical models developed to describe the nature of social behaviour, the stimulus–response model (in which every social act is seen as a response to the preceding act of another individual) has been generally found helpful but incomplete. Linguistic models that view social behaviour as being governed by principles analogous to the rules of a game or specifically to the grammar of a language have also attracted adherents. Others see social behaviour as a kind of motor skill that is goal-directed and modified by feedback (or learning), while other models have been based on the theory of games, which emphasizes the pursuit and exchange of rewards and has led to experiments based on laboratory games. Not all small social groups function according to the same principles, and, indeed, modes of social activity vary for particular kinds of groups (e.g., for families, groups of friends, work groups, and committees).

Earlier research was concerned with whether small groups did better than individuals at various tasks (e.g., factory work), while later research has been directed more toward the study of interaction patterns among members of such groups. In the method known as sociometry, members nominate others (e.g., as best friends) to yield measures of preference and rejection in groups. Others have studied the effects of democratic and authoritarian leadership in groups and have greatly extended this work in industrial settings. In research on how people respond to group norms (e.g., of morality or of behaviour), most conformity has been found to the norms of reference groups (e.g., to such groups as families or close friends that are most important for people). The emergence and functioning of informal group hierarchies, the playing of social roles (e.g., leader, follower, scapegoat), and cohesiveness (the level of attraction of members to the group) have all been extensively studied. Experiments have been done on processes of group problem solving and decision making, the social conditions that produce the best results, and the tendency for groups to make risky decisions. Statistical field studies of industrial work groups have sought the conditions for greatest production effectiveness and job satisfaction.

Such organizations as businesses and armies have been studied by social surveys, statistical field studies, field experiments, and laboratory experiments on replicas of their social hierarchies and communication networks. Although they yield the most direct evidence, field experiments present difficulties, since the leaders and members of such organizations may effectively resist the intervention of experimenters. Clearly, efforts to try out democratic methods in a dictatorship are likely to be severely punished. Investigators can study the effects of role conflict resulting from conflicting demands (e.g., those from above and below) and topics such as communication patterns in social organizations. Researchers also have studied the sources of power and how it can be used and resisted. They consider the effectiveness of different organizational structures, studying variations in size, span of control, and the amount of power delegation and consultation. In factories, social psychologists study the effects of technology and the design of alternative work-flow systems. They investigate methods of bringing about organizational change (e.g., in the direction of improving the social skills of people and introducing industrial democracy).

Ways of looking at working organizations have changed considerably since 1900. Classical organization theory was criticized for its emphasis on social hierarchy, economic motivation, division of labour, and rigid and impersonal social relations. Later investigators emphasized the importance of flexibly organized groups, leadership skills, and job satisfaction based on less tangible rewards than salary alone. There has been a rather uneasy balance in the industrial social psychologist's concern with production and concern with people.

It is evident that there are individual differences in social behaviour; thus, people traditionally have been distinguished in terms of such personality traits as extroversion or dominance. Some personality tests are used to predict how an individual is likely to behave in laboratory discussion groups, but usually the predictive efficiency is very small. Whether or not an individual becomes a leader of a group, for example, is found to depend very little on what such personality tests measure and more on his skills in handling the group task compared with the skills of others. Indeed, the same person may be a leader in some groups and a follower in others. Similar considerations apply to other aspects of social behaviour, such as conformity, persuasibility, and dependency. Although people usually perceive others as being consistent in exhibiting personality traits, the evidence indicates that each individual may behave very differently, depending on the social circumstances.

The process by which personality is formed as the result of social influences is called socialization. Early research methods employed case studies of individuals and of individual societies (e.g., primitive tribes). Later research has made statistical comparisons of numbers of persons or of different societies; differences in child-rearing methods from one society to another, for example, have been shown to be related to the subsequent behaviour of the infants when they become adults. Such statistical approaches are limited since they fail to discern whether both the personality of the child and the child-rearing methods used by the parents are the result of inherited factors or whether the parents are affected by the behaviour of their children.

Problems in the process of socialization that have been studied by experimental methods include the analysis of mother–child interaction in infancy; the effects of parental patterns of behaviour on the development of intelligence, moral behaviour, mental health, delinquency, self-image, and other aspects of the personality of the child; the effects of birth order (e.g., being the first-born or second-born child) on the individual; and changes of personality during adolescence. Investigators have also studied the origins and functioning of achievement motivation and other social drives (e.g., as measured with personality tests).

Several theories have stimulated research into socialization; Freudian theory led to some of the earliest studies on such activities as oral and anal behaviour (e.g., the effect of the toilet training of children on obsessional and other "anal" behaviour). Learning theory led to the study of the effects of rewards and punishments on simple social behaviour and was extended to more complex processes such as imitation and morality (e.g., the analysis of conscience).

Such concepts as self-esteem, self-image, and ego-involvement have been regarded by some social psychologists as useful, while others have regarded them as superfluous. There is a considerable amount of research on such topics as embarrassment and behaviour in front of audiences, in which self-image and self-esteem have been assessed by various self-rating methods. The origin of awareness of self has been studied in relation to the reactions of others and to the child's comparisons of himself with other children. Particular attention has been paid to the so-called identity crisis that is observed at various stages of life (e.g., in adolescence) as the person struggles to discern the social role that best fits his self-concept.

Research into the origins, dynamics, and changes of attitudes and beliefs has been carried out by laboratory experiments (studying relatively minor effects), by social surveys and other statistical field studies, by psychometric studies, and occasionally by field experiments. The origins of these socially important predispositions have been sought in the study of parental attitudes, group norms, social influence and propaganda, and in various aspects of personality. The influence of personality has been studied by correlating measured attitudes with individual personality traits and by clinical studies of cognitive and motivational processes; so-called authoritarian behaviour, for example, has been found to be deeply embedded in the personality of the individual. Early research based on statistical analyses of social attitudes revealed correlations with such factors as radicalism–conservatism. Later research on consistency provided extensive laboratory evidence of consistency but little evidence of it in actual political behaviour (e.g., in attitudes on different political issues).

Research on attitude change has studied the effects of the mass media, the optimum design of persuasive messages, the effects of motivational arousal, and the role of opinion leaders (e.g., teachers and ministers). Research has been carried out into the origins, functioning, and change of particular attitudes (e.g., racial, international, political, and religious), each of which is affected by special factors. Attitudes toward racial minority groups, for example, are affected by social conditions, such as the local housing, employment, and the political situation; political attitudes are affected by social class and age; and religious attitudes and beliefs strongly reflect such factors as inner personality conflict.

CULTURAL THEORY

Finally, cultural theories of the 1930s emphasized human ability to innovate, accumulate, and diffuse culture. Heavily influenced by social and cultural anthropology, many sociologists concluded that culture was the most important factor in accounting for its own evolution and that of society. By 1940 cultural and social explanations of societal growth and change were accepted, with economic, geographic, and biopsychological factors playing subsidiary roles.

EARLY SCHOOLS OF THOUGHT

Scholars who established sociology as a legitimate social science were careful to distinguish it from biology and psychology, fields that had also begun to generalize about human behaviour. They did this by developing specific methods for the study of society.

EARLY FUNCTIONALISM

French sociologist Émile Durkheim (1858–1917), prominent in this regard, argued that various kinds of interactions between individuals bring about certain new properties (sui generis) not found in separate individuals. Durkheim insisted that these "social facts," as he called them—collective sentiments, customs, institutions, nations—should be studied and explained on a distinctly societal level (rather than on an individual level). To Durkheim the interrelations between the parts of society contributed to social unity—an integrated system with life characteristics of its own, exterior to individuals yet driving their behaviour. By positing a causal direction of social influence (from group to individual rather than the reverse, the model accepted by most biologists and psychologists of the time), Durkheim gave a much-needed framework to the new science of sociology. Some writers called this view "functionalism," although the term later acquired broader meanings.

Durkheim pointed out that groups can be held together on two contrasting bases: mechanical solidarity, a sentimental attraction of social units or groups that perform the same or similar functions, such as preindustrial self-sufficient farmers; or organic solidarity, an interdependence based on differentiated functions and specialization as seen in a factory, the military, government, or other complex organizations.

Other theorists of Durkheim's period made similar distinctions and predicted that civilization would progress along the lines of specialization and contractual relations. British legal historian Henry Maine, for example, used status and contract. German sociologist Ferdinand Tönnies's conception of the nature of social systems is based on his distinction between the *Gemeinschaft* (communal society) and the *Gesellschaft* (associational society). In the rural, peasant societies that typify the *Gemeinschaft*, personal relationships are defined and regulated on the basis of traditional social rules. People have simple and direct face-to-face relations with each other that are determined by *Wesenwille* (natural will)—i.e., natural and spontaneously arising emotions and expressions of sentiment. The *Gesellschaft*, in contrast, is the creation of *Kürwille* (rational will) and is typified by modern, cosmopolitan societies with their government bureaucracies and large industrial organizations. In the *Gesellschaft*, rational self-interest and calculating conduct act to weaken the traditional bonds of family, kinship, and religion that permeate the *Gemeinschaft*'s structure. In the *Gesellschaft*, human relations are more impersonal and indirect, being rationally constructed in the interest of efficiency or other economic and political considerations.

Later anthropologists, especially Bronisław Malinowski and A.R. Radcliffe-Brown, developed a doctrine of functionalism that emphasized the interrelatedness of all parts of society. They theorized that a change in any single element would produce a general disturbance in the whole society.

As one of the most intellectually vigorous social scientists of his day, Malinowski had a stimulating and wide influence. His seminars were famous, and he attracted the attention of prominent scientists in other disciplines, such as linguistics and psychology, and collaborated or debated with them. He favoured an approach that focused more on the individual—an approach that seemed to him more realistic. His functional theory, as he himself explained,

> **insists . . . upon the principle that in every type of civilisation, every custom, material object, idea and belief fulfils some vital function, has some task to accomplish, represents**

Émile Durkheim

an indispensable part within a working whole. ("Anthropology," in *Encyclopædia Britannica,* 13th ed., suppl., p. 133.)

Only by understanding such functions and interrelations, Malinowski held, can an anthropologist understand a culture. In keeping with his concept of culture as an expression of the totality of human achievement, he examined a wide range of cultural aspects and institutions, challenging existing interpretations of kinship and marriage, exchange, and ritual.

This doctrine eventually gained such a following among social anthropologists that some advocated a policy of complete noninterference, even with objectionable practices in preliterate societies (such as cannibalism or head-hunting), for fear that eliminating the practice might produce far-reaching social disorganization.

Functionalism also postulates that all cultural or social phenomena have a positive function and that all are indispensable. Distinctions have been made between manifest functions, those consequences intended and recognized by participants in the system, and latent functions, which are neither intended nor recognized.

In an attempt to develop a more dynamic analysis of social systems, the American sociologist Talcott Parsons introduced a

ÉMILE DURKHEIM

A pioneering social scientist, Émile Durkheim (1858–1917) is widely regarded as the founder of the French school of sociology.

Born in Épinal, France, Durkheim studied philosophy at the prestigious École Normale Supérieure in Paris. Upon graduation in 1882 he taught in secondary schools until he was appointed to a lectureship especially founded for him at the University of Bordeaux. This was the first course of social science officially provided in a French university.

Durkheim's doctoral thesis, *The Division of Labor in Society*, published in 1893, focused on the problems of new technology and the mechanization of work. This division of labor, according to Durkheim, made workers both more alien to one another, as their jobs were different, and more dependent on one another, as none any longer built the whole of a product. The methods to be used to examine society in this new discipline Durkheim laid out in *The Rules of Sociological Method* (1895).

His classic *Suicide* (1897) examined the ties that bind individuals to the society in which they live—and their breakdown. Suicide appeared to be more frequent in societies where individuals are less a part of the life around them, as in modern industrial societies. He distinguished three types of suicide: In egoistic suicide the individual shuts himself off from other human beings. Anomic suicide comes from the belief that the world has fallen apart around one. Altruistic suicide springs from great loyalty to a cause.

structural–functional approach that employs the concept of function as a link between relatively stable structural categories. Any process or set of conditions that does not contribute to the maintenance or development of the system is said to be dysfunctional. In particular, there is a focus on the conditions of stability, integration, and effectiveness of the system.

THE FUNCTIONALIST-CONFLICT DEBATE

American sociology began undergoing significant development in the 1940s. The monumental growth of university enrollment and research after World War II was fueled by generous federal and private funding of research. Sociologists sought to enhance their status as scientists by pursuing empirical research and by conducting qualitative analysis of significant social problems. Many universities developed large research organizations that spurred important advances in survey research application, measurement, and social statistics. At the forefront were Columbia University (focusing on cultural surveys) and the University of Chicago (specializing in quantitative analysis of social conditions and detailed studies of urban problems). The struggle over the meaningful use of statistics and theory in research began at this time and remained a continuing debate in the discipline.

The gap between empirical research and theory persisted, in part because functionalist theory seemed divorced from the empirical research programs that defined mid-20th-century sociology. Functionalism underwent some modification when sociologist Talcott Parsons enunciated the "functional prerequisites" that any social system must meet in order to survive: developing routinized interpersonal arrangements, defining relations to the external environment, fixing boundaries, and recruiting and controlling members. Along with Robert K. Merton and others, Parsons classified such structures on the basis of their functions. This approach,

Ferdinand Tönnies

called structural-functional analysis (and also known as systems theory), was applied so broadly that Marion Levy and Kingsley Davis suggested it was synonymous with the scientific study of social organization.

That structural-functional emphasis changed in the 1960s, however, with new challenges to the functionalist notion that a society's survival depended on institutional practices. This belief, along with the notion that the stratification system selected the most talented and meritorious individuals to meet society's needs, was seen by some as a conservative ideology that legitimated the status quo and thereby prevented social reform. It also ignored the potential of the individual within society. In a response to the criticism of structural-functionalism, some sociologists proposed a "conflict sociology." In this view, the dominant institutions repress the weaker groups. This view gained prominence in the United States with the social turmoil of the civil rights struggle and the Vietnam War over the 1960s and '70s and prompted many younger sociologists to adopt this neo-Marxist view. Their interpretation of class conflict seemed consistent with the principal tenet of general conflict theory: that conflict pervades all of society, including the family, the economy, polity, and education.

STRUCTURAL FUNCTIONALISM

A.R. Radcliffe-Brown connected function to social structure. In his view, the components of the social structure have indispensable functions for one another—the continued existence of the one component is dependent on that of the others—and for the society as a whole, which is seen as an integrated, organic entity. His comparative studies of preliterate societies demonstrated that the interdependence of institutions regulated much of social and individual life. Radcliffe-Brown defined social structure empirically as patterned, or "normal," social relations (those aspects of social activities that conform to accepted social rules or norms). These rules bind society's members to socially useful activities.

Talcott Parsons elaborated on the work of Durkheim and Radcliffe-Brown in formulating a theory that was valid for large and complex societies. For Parsons, social structure was essentially normative—that is, consisting of "institutional patterns of normative culture." Put differently, social behaviour conforms to norms, values, and rules that direct behaviour in specific situations. These norms vary according to the positions of the individual actors: they define different roles, such as various occupational roles or the roles of husband-father and wife-mother. Moreover, these norms vary among different spheres of life and lead to the creation of social institutions—for example, property and marriage. Norms, roles, and institutions are all components of the social structure on different levels of complexity.

THEORIES OF CLASS AND POWER

Parsons's work has been criticized for several reasons, not least for the comparatively meagre attention he paid to inequalities of power, wealth, and other social rewards. Other social theorists, including functionalists such as Robert K. Merton, have given these "distributional" properties a more central place in their concepts of society. For Merton and others, the structure of society consists not only of normative patterns but also of the inequalities of power, status, and material privileges, which give the members of a society widely different opportunities and alternatives.

In complex societies, these inequalities define different strata, or classes, that form the stratification system, or class structure, of the society. Both aspects of the social structure, the normative and the distributive aspect, are strongly interconnected, as may be inferred from the observation that members of different classes often have different and even conflicting norms and values.

This leads to a consideration contrary to structural functionalism: certain norms in a society may be established not because of any general

TALCOTT PARSONS

Talcott Parsons (1902–1979) was an American sociologist and scholar whose theory of social action influenced the intellectual bases of several disciplines of modern sociology. His work is concerned with a general theoretical system for the analysis of society rather than with narrower empirical studies. He is credited with having introduced the work of Max Weber and Vilfredo Pareto to American sociology.

After receiving his B.A. from Amherst College in 1924, Parsons studied at the London School of Economics and at the University of Heidelberg, where he received his Ph.D. in 1927. He joined the faculty of Harvard University as an instructor in economics and began teaching sociology in 1931. In 1944 he became a full professor, and in 1946 he was appointed chairman of the new department of social relations, a post Parsons held until 1956. He remained at Harvard until his retirement in 1973. Parsons also served as president of the American Sociological Society in 1949.

Parsons united clinical psychology and social anthropology with sociology, a fusion still operating in the social sciences. His work is generally thought to constitute an entire school of social thought. In his first major book, *The Structure of Social Action* (1937), Parsons drew on elements from the works of several European scholars (Weber, Pareto, Alfred Marshall, and Émile Durkheim) to develop a common systematic theory of social action based on a voluntaristic principle—i.e., the choices between alternative values and actions must be at least partially free. Parsons defined the locus of sociological theory as residing not in the internal field of personality, as postulated by Sigmund Freud and Weber, but in the external field of the institutional structures developed by society. In *The Social System* (1951), he turned his analysis to large-scale systems and the problems of social order, integration, and equilibrium. He advocated a structural-functional analysis, a study of the ways in which the interrelated and interacting units that form the structures of a social system contribute to the development and maintenance of that system.

consensus about their moral value but because they are forced upon the population by those who have both the interest in doing so and the power to carry it out. To take one example, the "norms" of apartheid in South Africa reflected the interests and values of only one section of the population, which had the power to enforce them upon the majority. In theories of class and power, this argument has been generalized: norms, values, and ideas are explained as the result of the inequalities of power between groups with conflicting interests.

The most influential theory of this type has been Marxism, or historical materialism. The Marxian view is succinctly summarized in Marx's phrase, "The ideas of the ruling class are, in every age, the ruling ideas." These ideas are regarded as reflections of class interests and are connected to the power structure, which is identified with the class structure. This Marxian model, which was claimed to be particularly valid for capitalist societies, has met with much criticism. One basic problem is its distinction between economic structure and spiritual superstructure, which are identified with social being and consciousness, respectively. This suggests that economic activities and relations are in themselves somehow independent of consciousness, as if they occur independently of human beings.

Nevertheless, the Marxian model became influential even among non-Marxist social scientists. The distinction between material structure and nonmaterial superstructure continues to be reflected in sociological textbooks as the distinction between social structure and culture. Social structure here refers to the ways people are interrelated or interdependent; culture refers to the ideas, knowledge, norms, customs, and capacities that they have learned and share as members of a society.

STRUCTURALISM

Another important theoretical approach is structuralism (sometimes called French structuralism), which studies the underlying, unconscious regularities of human expression—that is, the unobservable structures that have observable effects on behaviour, society, and culture. French anthropologist Claude Lévi-Strauss derived this theory from structural linguistics, developed by the Swiss linguist Ferdinand de Saussure. According to Saussure, any language is structured in the sense that its elements are interrelated in nonarbitrary, regular, rule-bound ways; a competent speaker of the language largely follows these rules without being aware of doing so. The task of the theorist is to detect this underlying structure, including the rules of transformation that connect the structure to the various observed expressions.

According to Lévi-Strauss, this same method can be applied to social and cultural life in general. He constructed theories concerning the underlying structure of kinship systems, myths, and customs of cooking and eating. The structural method, in short, purports to detect the common structure of widely different social and cultural forms. This structure does not determine concrete expressions, however; the variety of expressions it generates is potentially unlimited. Moreover, the structures that generate the varieties of social and cultural forms ultimately reflect, according to Lévi-Strauss, basic characteristics of the human mind.

Structures such as the human mind, grammar, and language are sometimes called "deep structures" or "substructures." Since such

Robert K. Merton

The Frankfurt School

The group of researchers associated with the Institute for Social Research in Frankfurt am Main, Germany, applied Marxism to a radical interdisciplinary social theory. The Institute for Social Research (Institut für Sozialforschung) was founded by Carl Grünberg in 1923 as an adjunct of the University of Frankfurt; it was the first Marxist-oriented research centre affiliated with a major German university. Max Horkheimer took over as director in 1930 and recruited many talented theorists, including T.W. Adorno, Erich Fromm, Herbert Marcuse, and Walter Benjamin.

The members of the Frankfurt School tried to develop a theory of society that was based on Marxism and Hegelian philosophy but which also utilized the insights of psychoanalysis, sociology, existential philosophy, and other disciplines. They used basic Marxist concepts to analyze the social relations within capitalist economic systems. This approach, which became known as "critical theory," yielded influential critiques of large corporations and monopolies, the role of technology, the industrialization of culture, and the decline of the individual within capitalist society. Fascism and authoritarianism were also prominent subjects of study. Much of this research was published in the institute's journal, *Zeitschrift für Sozialforschung* (1932–41; "Journal for Social Research").

Most of the institute's scholars were forced to leave Germany after Adolf Hitler's accession to power (1933), and many found refuge in the United States. The Institute for Social Research thus became affiliated with Columbia University until 1949, when it returned to Frankfurt. In the 1950s the critical theorists of the Frankfurt School diverged in several intellectual directions. Most of them disavowed orthodox Marxism, though they remained deeply critical of capitalism. Marcuse's critique of what he perceived as capitalism's increasing control of all aspects of social life enjoyed unexpected influence in the 1960s among the younger generation. Jürgen Habermas emerged as the most prominent member of the Frankfurt School in the postwar decades, however. He tried to open critical theory to developments in analytic philosophy and linguistic analysis, structuralism, and hermeneutics.

structures are not readily observable, they must be discerned from intensive interpretive analysis of myths, language, or texts. Then they can be applied to explain the customs or traits of social institutions. French philosopher Michel Foucault, for example, used this approach in his study of corporal punishment. His research led him to conclude that the abolition of corporal punishment by liberal states was an illusion because the state substituted punishment of the "soul" by monitoring and controlling both the behaviour of prisoners and the behaviour of everyone in the society.

Structuralism became an intellectual fashion in the 1960s in France, where writers as different as Roland Barthes, Foucault, and Louis Althusser were regarded as representatives of the new theoretical current. In this broad sense, however, structuralism is not one coherent theoretical perspective. The Marxist structuralism of Althusser, for example, is far removed from the anthropological structuralism of Lévi-Strauss. The structural method, when applied by different scholars, appears to lead to different results.

The onslaught of criticism launched against structural functionalism, class theories, and structuralism indicates the problematic nature of the concept of social structure. Yet the notion of structure is not easy to dispense with because it expresses ideas of continuity, regularity, and interrelatedness in social life.

RISING SEGMENTATION OF THE DISCIPLINE

The early schools of thought each presented a systematic formulation of sociology that implied possession of exclusive truth and that involved a conviction of the need to destroy rival systems. By 1975 the era of growth, optimism, and surface consensus in sociology had come to an end. The functionalist-conflict debate signaled further and permanent divisions in the discipline, and virtually all textbooks presented it as the main theoretical divide, despite Lewis A. Coser's widely known proposition that social conflict, while divisive, also has an integrating and stabilizing effect on society. Conflict is not necessarily negative, argued Coser in *The Functions of Social Conflict* (1936), because it can ultimately foster social cohesiveness by identifying social problems to be overcome. In the late 1970s, however, attention to other, everyday social processes such as those elaborated by the Chicago School (competition, accommodation, and assimilation) ceased appearing in textbooks. In its extreme form, conflict theory helped revive the critical theory of the Frankfurt School that wholly rejected all sociological theories of the time as proponents of the status quo. These theoretical divisions themselves became institutionalized in the study and practice of sociology, which suggested that debates on approach would likely remain unresolved.

CHAPTER FIVE

MAJOR MODERN DEVELOPMENTS

One of the consequences of the functionalist-conflict divide, recognized by the 1970s as unbridgeable, was a decline in general theory building. Others were growing specialization and controversy over methodology and approach. Communication between the specialties also diminished, even as ideological disputes and other disagreements persisted within the specialty areas. New academic journals were introduced to meet the needs of the emerging specializations, but this further obscured the core of the discipline by causing scholars to focus on microsociological issues. Interestingly, theory building grew within the specialties—fractured as they were—especially as international comparative research increased contact with other social sciences.

SOCIAL STRATIFICATION

Since social stratification is the most binding and central concern of sociology, changes in the study of social stratification reflect trends in the entire discipline. The founders of sociology thought that the United States, unlike Europe, was a classless society with a high degree of upward mobility. During the Great Depression, however, Robert and Helen Lynd, in their famous Middletown (1937) studies, documented the deep divide between the working and the business classes in all areas of community life. (On the basis of field observations of social stratification in Muncie, Indiana, the Lynds wrote "Middletown: A Study in Contemporary American Culture"

(1929), innovatively treating the middle class as a tribe in the anthropological sense. Their follow-up study, "Middletown in Transition: A Study in Cultural Conflicts" (1937), analyzed the social changes induced by the Great Depression of the 1930s.) W. Lloyd Warner and colleagues at Harvard University applied anthropological methods to study the *Social Life of a Modern Community* (1941) and found six social classes with distinct subcultures: upper upper and lower upper, upper middle and lower middle, and upper lower and lower lower classes. In 1953 Floyd Hunter's study of Atlanta, Georgia, shifted the emphasis in stratification from status to power; he documented a community power structure that controlled the agenda of urban politics. Likewise, C. Wright Mills in 1956 proposed that a "power elite" dominated the national agenda in Washington, a cabal comprising business, government, and the military.

From the 1960s to the 1980s, research in social stratification was influenced by the attainment model of stratification, initiated at the University of Wisconsin by William H. Sewell. Designed to measure how individuals attain occupational status, this approach assigned each occupation a socioeconomic score and then measured the distance between sons' and fathers' scores, also using the educational achievement of fathers to explain intergenerational mobility. Peter M. Blau and Otis Dudley Duncan used this technique in the study published as *The American Occupational Structure* (1967). The study advanced scientific understanding of the structure and development of work-related mobility patterns in the United States. It was the first national intergenerational survey to represent the influences of family background, education, race, region, size of community, and other factors on the occupational mobility of men. The book received the Sorokin Award of the American Sociological Association.

Attempting to build a general theory, Gerhard Lenski shifted attention to whole societies and proposed an evolutionary theory in *Power and Privilege* (1966), demonstrating that the dominant forms of production (hunting and gathering, horticulture, agriculture, and industry) were consistently associated with particular systems of

C. Wright Mills

Charles Wright Mills (1916–1962) was an American sociologist who, with Hans H. Gerth, applied and popularized Max Weber's theories in the United States. He joined the sociology faculty at Columbia University in 1946. At Columbia, Mills promoted the idea that social scientists should not merely be disinterested observers engaged in research and theory but assert their social responsibility. He was concerned about the ethics of his sociological peers, feeling that they often failed to affirm moral leadership and thus surrendered their social responsibility and allowed special interests, or people lacking qualifications, to assume positions of leadership.

Mills's work drew heavily from Weber's differentiation between the various impacts of class, status, and power in explaining stratification systems and politics. His analysis of the major echelons of American society appeared in "The New Men of Power, America's Labor Leaders" (1948), "White Collar" (1951), and his best-known work, "The Power Elite" (1956). In this last book, Mills located the "elite," or ruling class, among those business, government, and military leaders whose decisions and actions have significant consequences.

stratification. This theory was enthusiastically accepted, but only by a minority of sociologists. Addressing the contemporary world, Marion Levy theorized in *Modernization and the Structures of Societies* (1960) that underdeveloped nations would inevitably develop institutions that paralleled those of the more economically advanced nations, which ultimately would lead to a global convergence of societies. Challenging the theory as a conservative defense of the West, Immanuel Wallerstein's

Robert S. Lynd

The Modern World System (1974) proposed a less-optimistic world-system theory of stratification. Wallerstein averred that advanced industrial nations would develop most rapidly and thereby widen global inequality by holding the developing nations in a permanent state of dependency.

Having been challenged as a male-dominated approach, traditional stratification theory was massively reconstructed in the 1970s to address the institutional gender inequalities found in all societies. Rae Lesser Blumberg, drawing on the work of Lenski and economist Esther Boserup, theorized the basis of persistent inequality in *Stratification, Socioeconomic, and Sexual Inequality* (1978). Janet Saltzman Chafetz took economic, psychological, and sociological factors into account in *Gender Equity: An Integrated Theory of Stability and Change* (1990). Traditional theories of racial inequality were challenged and revised by William Julius Wilson in *The Truly Disadvantaged* (1987). His book uncovered mechanisms that maintained segregation and disorganization in African American communities. Disciplinary specialization, especially in the areas of gender, race, and Marxism, came to dominate sociological inquiry.

For example, Eric Olin Wright, in *Classes* (1985), introduced a 12-class scheme of occupational stratification based on ownership, supervisory control of work, and monopolistic knowledge. Wright's book, an attack on the individualistic bias of attainment theory written from a Marxist perspective, drew on the traits of these 12 classes to explain income inequality. The nuanced differences between social groups were further investigated in *Divided We Stand* (1985) by William Form, whose analysis of labour markets revealed deep permanent fissures within working classes previously thought to be uniform.

Some investigative specializations, however, were short-lived. Despite their earlier popularity, ethnographic studies of communities, such as those by Hunter, Warner, and the Lynds, were increasingly abandoned in the 1960s and virtually forgotten by the 1970s. Intensive case studies of bureaucracies begun in the '70s followed a similar path. Like economists, sociologists have increasingly turned to large-scale surveys

C. Wright Mills

and government data banks as sources for their research. Social stratification theory and research continue to undergo change and have seen substantive reappraisal ever since the breakup of the Soviet system.

SOCIAL CLASS

The term "social class" refers to a group of people within a society who possess roughly the same socioeconomic status. Virtually all societies have some form of social ranking, though the nature of class distinctions varies around the globe. Sociologists generally view social classes as existing hierarchically, with those at the top enjoying certain advantages over the rest.

A person's social standing may be based on such factors as wealth, occupation, family relationships, ethnicity, religion, and level of education. The relative importance of these and other factors varies depending on the society. In the United States, for example, much less significance is attached to family relationships than in Great Britain, which has retained its hereditary aristocracy. The importance attached to a particular factor may also change over time. Historically, education was less significant as a determinant of social class in the United States than in many European countries. By the late 20th century, however, the decline in low-skilled jobs in the United States—combined with an increase in the number of jobs requiring a college degree—had strengthened the connection between socioeconomic status and level of education.

Class distinctions are nearly as old as organized human society. They became established through the exercise of power and the accumulation of wealth by a few members of society. Distinctions between the few and the many were then perpetuated by inheritance and by law. In the ancient world the few were society's rulers: kings and nobles, priests, and the military leadership. The many were the mass of citizens who did most of society's work. There was no group between these two social segments comparable to today's middle class.

William Julius Wilson

William Julius Wilson

William Julius Wilson (b. 1935) is an American sociologist whose views on race and urban poverty helped shape U.S. public policy and academic discourse. Wilson was educated at Wilberforce University and Bowling Green State University in Ohio, as well as at Washington State University. He joined the faculty of the University of Massachusetts (Amherst) as an assistant professor of sociology in 1965. In 1972 he moved to the University of Chicago, becoming a full professor in 1975 and gaining a chaired university professorship in 1990. Wilson conducted research, taught, wrote on inner-city poverty, and led the Center for the Study of Urban Inequality at the University of Chicago until 1996, when he joined Harvard University as a university professor in sociology and became the director of Harvard's Joblessness and Urban Poverty Research Program.

In two seminal works, *The Declining Significance of Race: Blacks and Changing American Institutions* (1978) and *The Truly Disadvantaged: The Inner City, the Underclass, and Public Policy* (1987), Wilson maintained that class divisions and global economic changes, more than racism, had created a large African American underclass. In *When Work Disappears: The World of the New Urban Poor* (1996), he showed how chronic joblessness deprived those in the inner city of skills necessary to obtain and keep jobs. In *More Than Just Race: Being Black and Poor in the Inner City* (2009) he addressed urban poverty among African Americans.

Wilson disputed the liberal stance that the "black underclass" (a term he later abandoned) owed its existence to entrenched racial discrimination; he also disagreed with the conservative view that African American poverty was due to cultural deficiencies and welfare dependency. Instead, Wilson implicated sweeping changes in the global economy that pulled low-skilled manufacturing jobs out of the inner city; the flight from the inner city of its most successful residents; and the lingering effects of past discrimination. He believed the problems of the underclass could be alleviated only by "race neutral" programs such as universal health care and government-financed jobs. Wilson was a MacArthur Prize fellow from 1987 to 1992, and he was awarded the National Medal of Science in 1998. In 2003 he received the American Academy of Arts and Sciences Talcott Parsons Prize for his contributions to the social sciences.

The most influential theoretician on social class was Karl Marx. Marx endeavored to show that history is defined by a continuous struggle among the various classes to control the means of economic production. By the mid-19th century this struggle was between the capitalists, who owned the means of production in industrialized societies, and the workers. Marx predicted that the workers would wrest control of production from the capitalists and that the end result would be a classless society.

Most subsequent theories of social class were responses to Marx's view. Early in the 20th century Max Weber made a distinction between class, status, and power. He argued that these three categories represent different forms of social hierarchy that do not necessarily coincide. Weber agreed with Marx that class is determined mainly by the ownership or nonownership of property. Status, however, is based on social honors, prestige, and style of living. Many modern celebrities, such as professional athletes and entertainers, have high status. They are not capitalists in the Marxist sense, but they win great popular approval and have the wealth to support their often exaggerated style of living. In Weber's third category, power, belong those who possess the means of command—the political and military segments.

Modern conceptions of social class tend to emphasize occupation or wealth. In general, sociologists group people into three classes: upper, working (or lower), and middle. An "underclass" of chronically jobless and underemployed workers is also frequently cited.

In contemporary industrialized societies, the upper class is distinguished mainly by its possession of great wealth—either inherited or earned. Such wealth enables those who possess it to enjoy distinctive personal and cultural pursuits from which most of the population is excluded. It also gives them a powerful influence on public policy.

The working class is a misleading term because most members of all classes engage in some kind of work. The name refers to those who are commonly called blue-collar workers. At one time, these were skilled and semiskilled laborers who worked primarily in mines and manufacturing industries. By the late 20th century, however, the large majority of blue-collar workers held jobs in service industries. As a class, these workers are traditionally distinguished by dependence on wages and lack of significant property holdings. Economic expansion following World War II propelled many working-class families into the middle class, but slower economies in the late 20th century increasingly restricted opportunities for economic mobility.

The largest population segment in modern industrial societies, the middle class is also the most varied. Some of its members would once have been considered blue-collar workers. Others, in what is called the upper middle class, have incomes and lifestyles that approximate those of the upper class. Generally, members of the middle class include professionals (lawyers, clergy, and physicians), teachers, farmers, small businesspeople, and others.

The term "underclass" refers to people who, from one generation to another, experience unusually high rates of unemployment. United States sociologist Oscar Lewis has asserted that a "culture of poverty," or a set of beliefs and practices adopted by members of the underclass, prevents these individuals from escaping poverty despite their desire to do so. Other sociologists have argued that it is external forces—racism, deteriorated schools, and a lack of jobs in inner cities, for example—that keep people in the underclass.

Members of the underclass are generally dependent on state assistance. Between 1996 and 2001, welfare reform in the United States reduced the number of aid recipients by about half, but the number of United States citizens living in poverty continued to rise. The numbers of the poor in Europe swelled at the end of the 20th century as aging populations and record unemployment overwhelmed state relief programs and as former Communist countries struggled to restructure their economies.

INTERDISCIPLINARY INFLUENCES

The significant growth of sociological inquiry after World War II prompted interest in historical and political sociology. Charles Tilly in *From Mobilization to Revolution* (1978), Jack Goldstone in *Revolutions: Theoretical, Comparative and Historical Studies* (1993), and Arthur Stinchcombe in *Constructing Social Theories* (1987) made comparative studies of revolutions and proposed structural theories to explain the origins and spread of revolution. Sociologists who brought international and historical perspectives to their study of institutions such as education, welfare, religion, the family, and the military were forced to reconsider long-held theories and methodologies. As was the case in almost all areas of specialization, new journals were founded.

Sociological specialties were enriched by contact with other social sciences, especially political science and economics. Political sociology, for example, studied the social basis of party voting and partisan politics, spurring comparison of decision-making processes in city, state, and national governments. Still, sociologists split along ideological lines, much as they had in the functionalist-conflict divide, with some reporting that decisions were made pluralistically and democratically and others insisting that decisions were made by economic and political elites. Eventually, voting and community power studies were abandoned by sociologists, and those areas were left largely to political scientists.

From its inception, the study of social movements looked closely at interpersonal relations formed in the mobilization phase of collective action. Beginning in the 1970s, scholars focused more deeply on the long-term consequences of social movements, especially on evaluating the ways such movements have propelled societal change. The rich area of historical and international research that resulted includes the study of social turmoil's influence on New Deal legislation; the rise, decline, and resurrection of women's rights movements; analysis of both failed and successful revolutions; the impact of government and other institutions on social movements; national differences in how social movements spur discontent; the response of nascent movements to political changes; and variations in the rates of growth and decline of movements over time and in different nations. In short, countering the general trend, social movement research became better integrated into other specialties, especially in political and organizational sociology.

Stratification studies and organizational sociology were broadened to include economic phenomena such as labour markets and the behaviour of businesses. Econometric methods were also introduced from economics. Thus, to predict income, sociologists would examine status variables (such as race, ethnicity, or gender) or group affiliations (looking at degree of unionization, whether groups are licensed or unlicensed, and the type of industry, community, or firm involved). Other economic variables tapped by sociologists include human capital (education, training, and experience) and economic segmentation. As a result of his interaction with economists, for example, James S. Coleman was the first sociologist since Parsons to build a comprehensive social theory. Coleman's

Foundations of Social Theory (1990), based on economic models, suggests that the individual makes rational choices in all phases of social life.

THE HISTORICAL DIVIDE: QUALITATIVE AND ESTABLISHMENT SOCIOLOGY

Paradoxically, American sociology, unlike its European counterpart, has been marked by an individualistic (psychological) orientation, even though early sociologists fought to establish a discipline distinct from psychology. Most specialized research in American sociology still uses the individual as the unit of analysis. The standard practice is to collect data from or about individuals, categorize their social characteristics into "groups," and relate them to other categories of individuals such as income classes, occupations, and age groups. These intergroup relations are often examined with complex statistical tools. This practice is not generally recognized as social-psychological in nature, yet neither is it regarded as social structural analysis. Only a minority of sociologists in fields such as demography, human ecology, and historical or comparative institutional study use actual groups, organizations, and social structures as units of analysis.

As the field developed in the United States, many early 20th-century sociologists rejected instinctivist psychology and the classical behaviourism of John B. Watson. One group, however, emphasized the study of individuals in an approach called symbolic interaction, which took root at the University of Chicago early in the 20th century and remains prominent in contemporary sociology. John Dewey, George H. Mead, and Charles H. Cooley argued that the self is the individual's internalization of the wider society as revealed through interaction, the accumulated perceptions of how others see them. In other words, the mind and human self are not innate human equipment but constructions of the "person" (the socialized individual) derived from experience and intimate interpersonal interaction in small groups. This constructed

James S. Coleman

American sociologist James S. Coleman (1926–1995) was a pioneer in mathematical sociology. His studies strongly influenced education policy in the United States. Coleman was influenced by the style and ability of Paul Lazarsfeld to stimulate creative problem solving, an influence demonstrated in two major works: *Introduction to Mathematical Sociology* (1964) and *Mathematics of Collective Action* (1973).

Coleman was a fellow at the Center for Advanced Study of Behavioral Science in Palo Alto, California (1955–56), and then served as assistant professor of sociology at the University of Chicago (1956–59). He was an associate and then a full professor in the department of social relations at Johns Hopkins University from 1959 to 1973 and then returned to Chicago as professor and senior study director at the National Opinion Research Center, which is the University of Chicago's counterpart to the Bureau of Applied Social Research at Columbia University.

Coleman's work had a far-reaching impact on government education policy and sparked repeated controversy. In 1966 Coleman presented a report to the U.S. Congress in which he concluded that poor black children did better academically in integrated middle-class schools. His findings provided the sociological underpinnings for the widespread busing of students to achieve racial balance in schools, a practice that met with strong resistance from parents in many areas. In 1975 Coleman rescinded his support of busing, concluding that it had encouraged the deterioration of public schools by encouraging white flight to avoid integration. In 1981 Coleman published a study of 75,000 high school students that stated that private and Catholic schools, with more emphasis on discipline and with higher expectations of performance, provided an education superior to that of public schools.

James S. Coleman

self, however changing, functions as a guide to social behaviour. Social reality is thus made up of constructed symbols and meanings that are exchanged with others through daily interaction.

William I. Thomas and Ellsworth Faris used symbolic interaction theory to guide their empirical research in the tradition of Robert E. Park and Ernest W. Burgess by using personal documents, life histories, and autobiographies. The two revealed how people attach meanings to their experience and to the broader social world. This research tradition was enriched after 1960 by several innovations. The most sophisticated small-group research was devised by Erving Goffman in *The Presentation of Self in Everyday Life* (1959). Goffman insisted that the most meaningful individual behaviour occurs in the chance, intimate encounters of each day. These encounters include greeting people, appearing in public, and reacting to the physical appearance of others. Such encounters have structures of their own that can be researched by carefully constructing the "frames" (points of reference) people use to interpret and "stage" interactions. The structures are thought to represent true reality as opposed to the artificially constructed concepts that sociologists impose on the subjects they study.

In *Studies in Ethnomethodology* (1967), Harold Garfinkel coined the term "ethnomethodology" to designate the methods individuals use in daily life to construct their reality, primarily through intimate exchanges of meanings in conversation. These constructions are available through new methods of conversational analysis, detailed or "thick" descriptions of behaviour, "interpretive frames," and other devices. Proponents of this view have favoured the work of earlier European phenomenology, *Verstehen* (historical understanding), and interpretive sociology. More recently, qualitative sociologists have drawn on French structuralism, poststructuralism, and postmodernism to emphasize ways the "deeper" sources of hidden meanings in culture and language can affect the behaviour of individuals or of whole societies.

Since World War II, sociology has exported much of its theory, methodology, and findings to other divisions of the university, sometimes to its disadvantage. The study of human relations and formal organizations was transferred to business schools. The study of socialization, institutions, and stratification was absorbed by departments of education. Outside the university, the empirical methods and sociological theory prompted government agencies to adopt a behavioral perspective. Economists widened the scope of their research by introducing social variables to the analysis of economic behaviour. In short, although contemporary sociology is divided, it remains a vibrant field whose innovations contribute to its own development and that of social science in general.

CHAPTER SIX

METHODOLOGICAL CONSIDERATIONS IN SOCIOLOGY

Much 19th-century sociology had no system for gathering and analyzing data, but over time the inadequacies of speculative methods became increasingly evident, as did the need for obtaining reliable and verifiable knowledge. Like his contemporaries, Herbert Spencer assembled vast stores of observations made by others and used these to illustrate and support generalizations he had already formulated. Early social surveys like those conducted by Charles Booth in a monumental series on the social problems of London produced masses of data without regard to their theoretical relevance or reliability. Frédéric Le Play made similar use of the French case studies he drew on for his extensive investigations of family budgets.

Early exploitation of statistical materials, such as official records of birth, death, crime, and suicide, provided only moderate advances in knowledge. Data were easily manipulated, often to support preconceived ideas (the status quo). Among the most successful of such studies was that on suicide rates by Durkheim in *Le Suicide* (1897). Moreover, his *Rules of Sociological Method* (1895) had begun to meet the standards of scientific inquiry. In gathering data on suicides, Durkheim considered the social characteristics of individuals (e.g., religious affiliation, rural-urban residence) that reflected the degree of their social integration in the community, and he related these variables statistically.

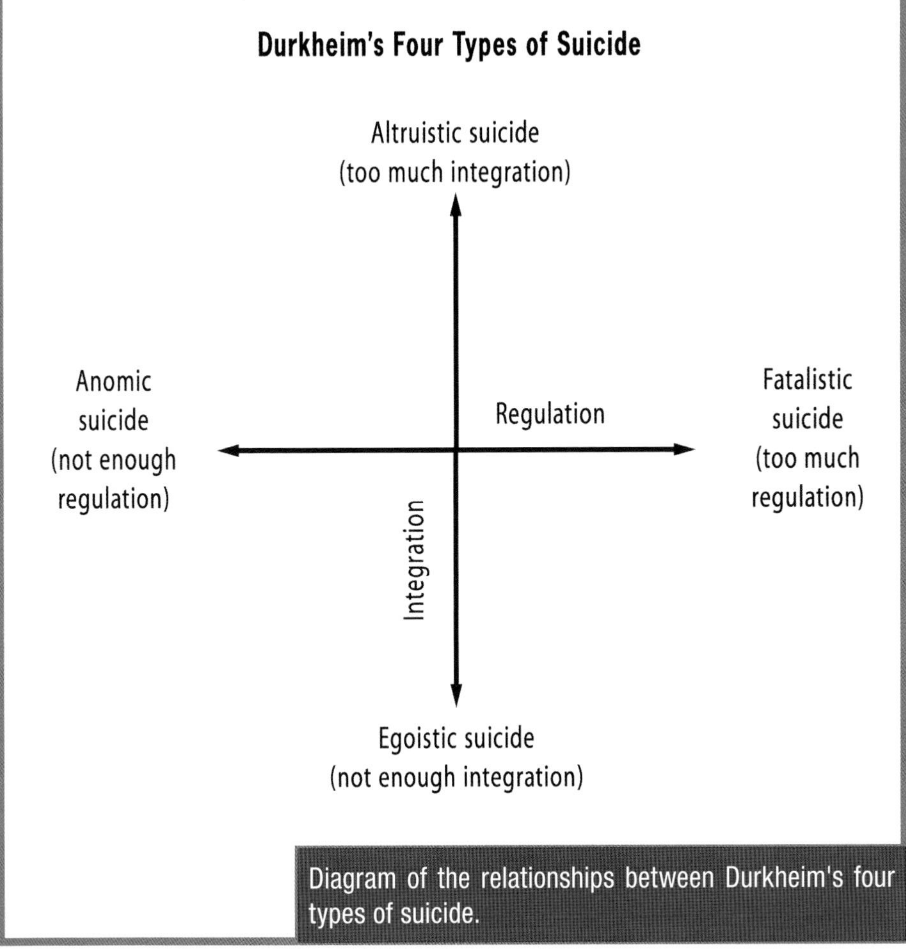

Diagram of the relationships between Durkheim's four types of suicide.

Durkheim's study of suicide was based on his observation that suicide appeared to be less frequent where the individual was closely integrated into a society; in other words, those lacking a strong social identification would be more susceptible to suicide. Thus, the apparently purely individual decision to renounce life could be explained through social forces.

It has been noted, at times with disapproval and amazement by non-French social scientists, that Durkheim traveled little and that, like many French scholars and the notable British anthropologist Sir James Frazer, he never undertook any fieldwork. The vast information Durkheim studied on the tribes of Australia and New Guinea and on the Eskimos was all collected by other anthropologists, travelers, or missionaries.

This was not due to provincialism or lack of attention to the concrete. Durkheim did not resemble the French philosopher Auguste Comte in making venturesome and dogmatic generalizations while disregarding empirical observation. He did, however, maintain that concrete observation in remote parts of the world does not always lead to illuminating views on the past or even on the present. For him, facts had no intellectual meaning unless they were grouped into types and laws. He claimed repeatedly that it is from a construction erected on the inner nature of the real that knowledge of concrete reality is obtained, a knowledge not perceived by observation of the facts from the outside. He thus constructed concepts such as the sacred and totemism exactly in the same way that Karl Marx developed the concept of class. In truth, Durkheim's vital interest did not lie in the study for its own sake of so-called primitive tribes but rather in the light such a study might throw on the present.

METHODOLOGICAL DEVELOPMENT IN CONTEMPORARY SOCIOLOGY

At the beginning of the 20th century, interest in developing a sociological methodology grew steadily. Methodological approaches outlined in W.I. Thomas and Florian Znaniecki's *Polish Peasant in Europe and America* (vol. 5, 1918–20) were recognized as an important advance, not so much in methodology as in committing sociologists to the task of improving methodology. Thomas and Znaniecki systematically gathered longitudinal data through letters, diaries, life histories, and other

Florian Znaniecki

Florian Znaniecki (1882–1958) was a Polish-American sociologist whose theoretical and methodological work helped make sociology a distinct academic discipline. He was a pioneer in the field of empirical investigation and was noted as an authority on Polish peasant culture.

Znaniecki's earliest work was as a poet. After being expelled from the University of Warsaw for his active support of Polish nationalism, he studied at various universities in France and Switzerland and received his doctorate in philosophy from the University of Kraków in 1909. Under the influence of the American sociologist W.I. Thomas, he turned to sociology, joining Thomas at the University of Chicago (1914), where they began their joint work, *The Polish Peasant in Europe and America,* 5 vol. (1918–20). This work made significant advances in methodology (notably in the use of intensive life histories) as well as in substance (a framework for the sociological view of personality and a study of immigrant social disorganization).

Znaniecki returned to Poland in 1920 and became professor of sociology at Pozna , where in 1922 he founded a sociological institute. He wrote several books in Polish, including an introduction to sociology and a work on the sociology of education; *The Laws of Social Psychology (1925)*; *The Method of Sociology* (1934); and *Social Actions* (1936). A series of lectures delivered at Columbia University was published as *The Social Role of the Man of Knowledge* (1940). The outbreak of World War II prevented Znaniecki's return to Poland, and he joined the faculty at the University of Illinois, Champaign-Urbana, where he wrote *Cultural Sciences, Their Origin and Development* (1952) and *Modern Nationalities* (1952).

relevant documents. Intended to gather specific data to help planners solve social problems, this approach soon became popular. The most ambitious of these "community social surveys" was the two-volume work *Great Depression, Recent Social Trends* (1933), edited by sociologists W.F. Ogburn and H.W. Odum.

Significant advances in scientific methodology occurred at the University of Chicago in the 1920s. Many studies of the metropolis and its subareas were conducted under the leadership of Robert E. Park, Ernest Burgess, and their colleagues. Most important, hypotheses were developed during the research rather than being imposed a priori (a practice later replaced by theoretically guided research). Many students took part in the studies and contributed to methods and findings.

ECOLOGICAL PATTERNING

A critical aspect of the Chicago School's urban research involved mapping locations. These included locations of land values, specific populations (racial, ethnic, or occupational), ethnic succession in neighbourhoods, residences of persons who committed certain crimes, or zones with a high incidence of divorce and desertion. Data-collection methods included participant observation, life histories, case studies, historical information, and life cycles of social movements. Sociologists at the University of Chicago paid equal attention to the improvement of methodology as they developed this approach. Here, for the first time, was a large-scale effort in which theory, methodology, and findings evolved together in an inductive process. Growing from its success in the American Midwest, urban research and zone mapping spread throughout the United States and influenced sociology abroad.

Ecological methods such as urban mapping were also first developed at Chicago, having grown out of the research on the metropolitan region, especially that regarding nonsocial patterns that resulted from the movement of populations, businesses, industries, residences, and institutions as each sought more advantageous locations. Most early urban studies

William Fielding Ogburn

American sociologist William Fielding Ogburn (1886–1959) was known for his application of statistical methods to the problems of the social sciences and for his introduction of the idea of "cultural lag" in the process of social change. Ogburn was a professor at Columbia University (1919–27) and the University of Chicago (1927–51). He frequently served as a labour mediator and was research director of the President's Research Committee on Social Trends (1930–33) during the administration of Herbert Hoover.

Ogburn's insistence on the verification of social theories by quantitative methods helped to shift the emphasis in sociology from social philosophy and reform programs toward the development of a more exact science of social phenomena. Ogburn considered what he termed invention—a new combination of existing cultural elements—to be the fundamental cause of social change and cultural evolution. Noting that an invention directly affecting one aspect of culture may require adjustments in other cultural areas, he introduced the term "cultural lag" to describe delays in adjustment to invention. Although lags are generally imperceptible over long periods of history, they may be so acute at a given moment as to threaten the complete disintegration of a society. For example, a major innovation in industrial processes may disrupt economics, government, and the social philosophy of a nation. In time, a new equilibrium will be established out of those disruptions. Among Ogburn's writings are "Social Change" (1922) and "Sociology" (1940; with Meyer F. Nimkoff).

mapped distributions that revealed relationships in general patterns of urban ecology. Because of this, multiple indicators of disorganization, stratification, vertical mobility, and population phenomena were found to follow regularities and could actually be considered predictable to some degree.

DEMOGRAPHY

Demography is the statistical study of human populations, especially with reference to size and density, distribution, and vital statistics (births, marriages, deaths, etc.). Contemporary demographic concerns include the "population explosion," the interplay between population and economic development, the effects of birth control, urban congestion, illegal immigration, and labour force statistics.

The roots of statistical demography may be found in the work of the Englishman John Graunt; his work *Natural and Political Observations... Made upon the Bills of Mortality* (1662) examines the weekly records of deaths and baptisms (the "bills of mortality") dating back to the end of the 16th century. In search of statistical regularities, Graunt made an estimate of the male-female ratios at birth and death-birth ratios in London and rural communities. His most celebrated contribution was his construction of the first mortality table; by analyzing birth and death rates he was able to estimate roughly the number of men currently of military age, the number of women of childbearing age, the total number of families, and even the population of London. Another such study was undertaken by Johann Süssmilch, whose *Die Göttliche Ordnung* (1741; "The Divine Order") analyzed the populations of 1,056 parishes in Brandenburg and various cities and provinces of Prussia. Süssmilch constructed several mortality tables, most notably the first such table for the whole population of Prussia (1765).

In 18th-century Europe, the development of life insurance and growing attention to public health produced an increased awareness of the significance of mortality studies. Civil registries of significant public events (births,

Howard Odum

Howard W. Odum (1884–1954) specialized in the social problems of the southern United States and was a pioneer of sociological education in the South. He worked to replace the Southern sectionalism with a sophisticated regional approach to social planning, race relations, and the arts, especially literature. A student of folk sociology, particularly that of southern blacks, he was ahead of his time in urging equal opportunity for African Americans.

Odum studied under noted psychologist G. Stanley Hall at Clark University and sociologist Franklin H. Giddings at Columbia University. In 1920 he joined the faculty of the University of North Carolina, where he established departments of sociology and public welfare, started a social-science research institute, and founded the journal *Social Forces*.

One of Odum's books on African Americans, *Rainbow Round My Shoulder: The Blue Trail of Black Ulysses* (1928), was praised for its literary quality. Among his other works are *Southern Regions of the United States* (1936), *Understanding Society* (1947), and *American Sociology* (1951). At President Herbert Hoover's request, Odum and William Fielding Ogburn edited the report *Recent Social Trends in the United States,* 2 vol. (1933), for the President's Research Committee on Social Trends.

deaths, and marriages) began in the 19th century to supplant church registries. Censuses of the population also developed during the 19th century.

For most of the 19th century, demographic studies continued to emphasize the phenomenon of mortality; it was not until demographers noted that a considerable decline of fertility had taken place in the industrialized countries during the second half of the 19th century, that they began to study fertility and reproduction with as much interest as they studied mortality. The phenomenon of differential fertility, with its implications about selection and more particularly about the evolution of intelligence, evoked widespread interest as shown in Charles Darwin's theories and in the works of Francis Galton. During the period between the two world wars, demography took on a broader, interdisciplinary character. In 1928 the International Union for the Scientific Study of Population was founded.

In spite of increasing sophistication in the analysis of statistics and the proliferation of research institutes, periodicals, and international organizations devoted to the science of demographics, the basis for most demographic research continues to lie in population censuses and the registration of vital statistics. Even the most meticulously gathered census is not completely accurate, however, and birth, death, and marriage statistics—based on certificates drawn up by local authorities—are accurate mostly in countries with a long tradition of registry.

EXPERIMENTS

Experimental methods, once limited to the domain of psychologists and considered inapplicable to social research, were eventually applied to the study of groups. By the 1930s, social psychologists Kurt Lewin, Muzafer Sherif, and their colleagues had begun conducting experiments on social interaction.

As a rule, successful experiments tend to occur in simple situations in which the variables are limited or controlled. Complex experiments, however, are possible. At Stanford, for example, a series of experiments over 30 years contributed to a formal theory of social status building and maintenance set forth by Joseph Berger and Morris Zelditch in *Status, Rewards, and Influence* (1985). At the University of Iowa, two decades of laboratory and computer-simulated research on power and exchange in small groups advanced theory in networks and decision making summarized by Barry Markovsky in *Social Psychology of Small Groups* (1993).

STATISTICS AND MATHEMATICAL ANALYSIS

Sociologists have increasingly borrowed statistical methods from other disciplines. Statistician Karl Pearson's "coefficient of correlation," for example, introduced an important concept for measuring associations between continuous variables without defining the nature of the connection. Later, statistical estimates of causal relations were probed by "multiple regression analysis," employing techniques that estimate the degree to which any particular variable influences a particular outcome.

Kurt Lewin

Patterns of responses to interview questions, once thought to be purely qualitative, have also been subject to mathematical scaling. A method devised by psychologist L.L. Thurstone in the late 1920s gained popular use in sociology. In this approach a list of items is presented to a number of judges who individually relist them in order of importance or of interest.

Items on which there is substantial agreement are then reordered to form a scale. Another technique asks participants to respond to statements by strength of agreement (strongly agree, agree, neither agree nor disagree, disagree, or strongly disagree). Social distance may be measured by asking respondents whether they would accept members of other groups as spouses, close friends, fellow employees, neighbours, or citizens.

A method called sociometry, introduced by J.L. Moreno in the 1930s, collects and tabulates information on group interactions. The interactions studied can appear trivial—for example, who confides in whom, which friends eat lunch together—or they may be more businesslike, such as who might be appointed as a group spokesperson. The data may be gathered by direct observation, interviews, or questionnaires. The preferences each individual has for specific others are then mapped with arrows from sender to receiver, and this results in a diagram of choices for the entire group. The person chosen most often is labeled a "star"; the person receiving no choices is called an "isolate."

The patterns may be quantified and supplemented with other data to reveal a group's informal structure. A powerful application of the approach, often mathematized, called network analysis, maps different types of interactions between organizations over extended periods and thus exposes a substructure not revealed from organizational charts or public documents.

Factor analysis, an elaboration of Pearson's coefficient of correlation, significantly reduces the number of complex variables to be considered. For instance, 50 different questions or measures of work alienation may in fact represent only seven or eight dimensions of alienation. Factor analysis reduces the variables to a more practical number of common factors and then determines each factor's relative contribution to the outcome variables.

Many other statistical methods have been devised to suit the purposes of such specialties as demography, ecology, social stratification, organizational analysis, mass communication, and social movements. Statistical methods have developed so rapidly that they sometimes

Sociometry

Sociometry refers to the measurement techniques used in social psychology, in sociology, and sometimes in social anthropology and psychiatry based on the assessment of social choice and interpersonal attractiveness. The term is closely associated with the work of the Austrian-born psychiatrist J.L. Moreno, who developed the method as a research and therapeutic technique. Sociometry has come to have several meanings; it is most commonly applied to the quantitative treatment of preferential interpersonal relations, but it is also used to mean the quantitative treatment of all kinds of interpersonal relations. The emphasis may be psychological or sociological.

A sociometric measure assesses the attractions (or repulsions) within a given group. The basic technique involves asking all group members to identify specific persons within the group they would prefer (or would not prefer) to have as partners in a given activity. Many variations on this technique exist for studying different aspects of social preference. For example, a group's networking structure can be exposed through the sociometric technique of recording all interactions between group members. The technique can also be applied on larger scale to reveal interorganizational networks by treating organizations as individual units.

Much work has focused on the concept of sociometric status. This includes studies of leadership; of social adjustment, ranging from the sociometric isolate (or unchosen individual) to the sociometric star (or highly chosen); of the relationship between sociometric status and other personality variables, demographic variables, and intelligence; and of minority-group prejudice.

outstrip scholars' ability to find data worthy of their application. Computers have accelerated the application of complex measures that were previously limited by the amount of time required for performing the mathematics. Progress in measurement has been so significant that the American Sociological Association in 1969 established an annual volume entitled *Sociological Methodology.*

DATA COLLECTION

Research techniques depend on the social phenomena studied. Data-collection techniques differ from participant observation, content analysis, interviewing, and documentary analysis. In this approach each problem studied requires a specific unit of observation, be it an individual, an organization, a city, a relationship between units, or a statistical rate. Even the way a concept is defined can affect data collection. For instance, when measuring occupational mobility, the definition of occupation is critical.

Steps must be taken to collect valid data. Many obstacles can arise, especially on sensitive subjects such as alcohol consumption in a community that prohibits or looks down upon it. In this instance the problem of gathering valid data might be circumvented by counting liquor bottles in trash receptacles or in the town dump. Similarly, a decline in the number of fictional works checked out of libraries has been used to estimate television-watching habits. Unfortunately, questionnaires, while useful for gathering information from large numbers of respondents, are marked by methodological problems. The wording of questions must be intelligible to the uneducated or uninterested as well as to the sophisticated respondent. Topics that provoke resistance must be presented in a way that yields a complete and unbiased response while keeping the interviewee engaged with the questions.

In face-to-face interviewing, it may be necessary to consider the interviewer's sex or race, appearance, manner, and approach. Questions must be posed in a way that does not influence the response. Interviewers must have steps for handling resistance or refusal. Indirect questioning, for example, may yield information that respondents would hesitate to provide in answers to direct questioning. Because of this, information collected through "canned" telephone interviews often leads to lower-quality data and poorer response rates.

Sampling errors and bias both constitute a continuing concern, especially since so much sociological knowledge is derived from samples of a larger universe. Where bias cannot be controlled, its extent may sometimes be estimated by various methods, including intensive analysis of smaller samples. For example, the population undercount in the United States is well known, as are the methods to estimate its extent, but political obstacles prevent the U.S. Bureau of the Census from revealing the undercount. Possibilities for errors arise in every stage of research, and the methods for reducing them constitute a continuing program of study in sociology.

NATIONAL METHODOLOGICAL PREFERENCES

Research approaches vary from country to country. All the methods described above are used by sociologists around the world, but their relative popularity depends somewhat on the sources of funding for the research and the relevance the subject may have to a particular country's interests. Where agricultural problems are of critical importance, as in developing countries, rural sociology and community studies are generally popular, especially when they can be conducted inexpensively by one or a few investigators. In France, Italy, and several other European nations, industrial sociology is understandably important, much of it based on case studies of industries and the experiences of workers. Sociology in Britain, the Scandinavian countries, and Japan covers most of the fields mentioned above. For most western European countries, interest focuses on social stratification and its political implications.

Psychologist Philip Zimbardo used experimental methods to study the behaviour of those in power in his landmark Stanford Prison Experiment.

In fact, general differences between the sociologies of European countries and that of the United States were established early in the 20th century. The European approach favoured broad sociological theory based on philosophical methods, while the American approach favoured induction and empiricism. Such differences have diminished somewhat in recent years, with remaining disparities stemming in part from ways that this expensive research is funded.

Sociology in Russia and eastern European countries is also becoming more similar to its western counterparts. Research in the former Soviet-bloc nations, previously shaped by the concepts and methods of Marxist sociology, has shifted to approaches influenced by European and American sociology.

More important than national preference is the methodological divide between scientific sociology and applied sociology; scholars interested in applied sociology tend to deprecate the methods and findings of the scientific sociologists as either irrelevant or ideologically biased. Issues of ethics have also been raised, particularly regarding observations and experiments in which the privacy of subjects may be felt to be invaded.

Finally, the divide between mainstream sociologists and those devoted to qualitative analysis seems deep and unbridgeable. Qualitative sociologists feel that their work is underrecognized and marginalized, even though it deals more with social reality than does standard sociology. Classical sociologists, in turn, feel that qualitative work can be trivial, philosophical, ideologically driven, or difficult to research. In addition, some members of groups who feel exploited (women, blacks, homosexuals, and the working class) assert that social observations cannot be made by outsiders; they believe that only victims have true insight into other victims and that they alone are equipped to do meaningful research in these areas. Minorities and other groups that locate themselves at the margins of society sometimes come together—often by organizing movements within professional societies—to challenge "establishment sociologists." This results in the direction of more attention, funding, and research to the more highly focused topics.

CHAPTER SEVEN

THE STATUS OF CONTEMPORARY SOCIOLOGY

The Greek philosophers and their European successors discussed much of the subject matter of sociology without thinking of it as a distinct discipline. In the early 19th century, the subject matter of the social sciences was discussed under the heading of moral philosophy. Even after Comte introduced the word "sociology" in 1838, sociological studies were combined with other subjects for some 60 years. Not until universities undertook a commitment to the subject could one make a living as a full-time sociologist. This commitment had to be made first by scholars in other fields such as history and economics.

ACADEMIC STATUS

As early as 1876, at the newly established Johns Hopkins University, some sociology was taught in the department of history and politics. In 1889 at the University of Kansas, the word appeared in the title of the department of history and sociology. In 1890 at Colby College, historian Albion Small taught a course called sociology, as did Franklin H. Giddings in the same year at Bryn Mawr College. But the first real commitment to the creation of a field of sociology took place in 1892 at the then new University of Chicago, where the recently arrived Albion Small received permission to create a department of sociology—the first such in the world. Within two years sociology departments had been founded at Columbia, Kansas, and Michigan, and shortly thereafter they were begun at Yale, Brown, and many other universities. By the late 1890s

Albion Small

Albion W. Small (1854–1926) was a sociologist who won recognition in the United States for sociology as an academic discipline with professional standards. In 1892 he became the first professor of sociology in the United States, at the University of Chicago, where he organized the first U.S. sociology department. In 1895 he founded, and for the rest of his life edited, the *American Journal of Sociology,* the first U.S. periodical of consequence devoted to the subject.

Through his mother's family, Small was a distant relative of Abraham Lincoln. He received a theological education in New England, studied in Germany for two years, earned a doctorate at Johns Hopkins University in 1889, and from that year to 1892 served as president of Colby College, Waterville, Maine.

With a Chicago colleague, George E. Vincent, Small wrote what is considered the world's first sociology textbook, *An Introduction to the Study of Society* (1894). He called the attention of U.S. scholars to contemporary German-language social theories, particularly those of the Austrian soldier and philosopher Gustav Ratzenhofer, whose ideas strongly influenced Small's *General Sociology* (1905).

Small's own strictly sociological theories and methods soon became obsolete, but he had a more lasting effect on political and economic thought. In political science his conception of the state as a mediator of conflicting group interests was taken up by subsequent writers. The institutional school of economists was influenced by his attack on capitalism, *Between Eras from Capitalism to Democracy* (1913), for which he drew on the ideas of Karl Marx; Thorstein Veblen, the U.S. economist of dynamics analysis, and Werner Sombart, the German sociological economist.

The University of Chicago established the United States' first sociology department.

nearly all higher-educational institutions in the United States either had departments of sociology or offered courses in the subject.

In 1895 the *American Journal of Sociology* began publication at the University of Chicago; in time a large number of journals followed in many other countries. Ten years later the American Sociological Society was organized, also to be followed by a large number of national, regional, international, and specialized sociological organizations. These groups institutionalized the subject and continue to guide its directions and define its boundaries. Eventually in 1949 the International Sociological Association was established under the sponsorship of UNESCO, and Louis Wirth of the University of Chicago was elected its first president.

The American Journal of Sociology

A Bimonthly edited by the Sociological Faculty of the University of Chicago, with the advice of leading sociologists in America and Europe. ALBION W. SMALL, Editor-in-Chief

THE ONLY JOURNAL IN THE ENGLISH LANGUAGE DEVOTED PRIMARILY TO PURE SOCIOLOGY

$2.00 a year; single copies, 50 cents

THE sociologists are working on the clue that human association—or " the stream of life," as it was called a generation ago—is a process, made up of lesser processes, down to the vanishing of social relations in movements within the individual consciousness which make the problems of psychology.

The goal of the sociologists is a statement of life in terms of the ultimate processes which are working out through the different incidents of human experience.

Some of the sociologists prefer to describe their work as a return to the ideal of social study proposed by Adam Smith, but developed by him only in the economic division of human activities. In the philosophy of the author of *The Wealth of Nations* the activities prompted by the wealth interests were merely one of several departments of human pursuits. In his scheme, accordingly, economic science was only one of an indefinite number of social sciences which must be worked out and correlated in order to furnish an adequate chart of actual social processes. For nearly a century the economic fraction of social science was cultivated as though it were the whole. Sociology is not a rival of economics. It is essentially a method of investigation, with the aim of making the other social processes as intelligible as the economists have made the processes which terminate in the production of wealth.

This **Journal** is a medium of publication for both general and special studies of social relations, as they appear from this point of view.

Subscriptions filed immediately to begin January, 1907, will include the November, 1906, number free.

The University of Chicago Press (Dept. 16), CHICAGO and NEW YORK

Albion Small established the *American Journal of Sociology* in 1895.

The rapid increase of full-time sociologists, along with the growth of sociology publications, allowed the content of the discipline also to expand rapidly. Research grew throughout the 20th century at an accelerated pace, especially after World War II, partly because of strong financial support from foundations, government, commercial sources, and individuals. This period was also marked by the rising popularity of anthropology, and many universities formed joint anthropology-sociology departments. By the 1960s, however, growing interest in anthropology had resulted in the formation of separate anthropology departments at the larger research universities. At the same time, interest in sociological research continued to develop. By 1970 there were more than a dozen important sociological journals and an indefinite number of minor journals worldwide. Along with this growth came

Louis Wirth

Sociologist Louis Wirth (1897–1952) pioneered the study of urban problems. A noted teacher at the University of Chicago from 1926, Wirth blended empirical research and theory in his work and contributed to the emergence of sociology as a profession. Wirth was president (1947) of the American Sociological Society and first president (1949–52) of the International Sociological Association.

He was the chief author of *Our Cities: Their Role in the National Economy* (1937). Written in the name of the U.S. National Resources Committee, this volume was an important early attempt to outline a national urban policy based on the findings of the social sciences. He also wrote *The Ghetto* (1928); "Urbanism as a Way of Life" (1938), an article published in the *American Journal of Sociology* that became a classic; and many other papers, collected in *Community Life and Social Policy* (1956) and *Louis Wirth on Cities and Social Life* (1964).

a flourishing of research institutions—some affiliated with university departments and some independent—which allowed a small but increasing number of sociologists to pursue full-time research free from teaching responsibilities.

In France, where Comte and later Durkheim gave early impetus to sociology, sociological research developed in a number of fields. The two world wars slowed that development somewhat, but after 1945 a strong revival of interest in sociology took place, during which the French government established a number of research institutes in the social sciences parallel to those in the natural sciences, including several in Paris—notably the Centre d'Études Sociologiques, the Institut National d'Études Démographiques, and the Maison des Sciences de l'Homme. These government-funded institutes employ many full-time sociologists, some of them among the more prominent scholars in the nation. The growth of sociological research at French universities has been somewhat more conservative; the Sorbonne, for example, in 1970 had only one chair officially assigned to sociology. The University of Nanterre, however, established a department with four professorships.

German sociology had a strong base in the late 19th century and afterward, and the writings of Tönnies, Weber, Georg Simmel, and others had an international impact. By the early 1930s, however, official Nazi hostility had impeded German sociology's development, and by the time of World War II the Nazis had destroyed sociology as an academic subject. Immediately after the war a new generation of scholars, aided by visiting sociologists, imported the new empirical research methods and began to develop a style of German sociology much different from the earlier theoretical and philosophical traditions. At the University of Frankfurt, Max Horkheimer's Institut für Sozialforschung (social research), established by private financing before the war, was revived. The University of Cologne also established a department notable for its survey research. West German universities remained conservative for a time, but two newly created ones—the Free University of Berlin and the University of Constance—made sociology one of their major disciplines.

By 1970 most West German universities had at least one chair in sociology. National needs received special emphasis, including studies of unemployment, youth problems, and delinquency. A significant amount of German research also is published in such fields as rural sociology, political sociology, and the family.

Despite the early prominence of Herbert Spencer and L.T. Hobhouse, the leading universities of the United Kingdom virtually ignored sociology until the mid-20th century. Before World War II, Britain excelled in anthropology, especially in the study of the British Empire's nonwhite societies. British sociology concentrated on studies of the poor, and much of it was undertaken by people with experience in social work rather than social research. The major prewar sociology department, at the London School of Economics, prioritized social reform over

German sociologist Max Horkheimer (*center*) was an early director of the Frankfurt School.

scientific research. In the postwar period, however, a considerable revival of sociology took place; Oxford and Cambridge recognized the subject by creating positions for sociologists, and various new universities established chairs and departments. Significant work in Britain has emerged in such fields as population and demography, sociology of organization, politics and industry, social stratification, and general sociology. The Tavistock Institute of Human Relations in London has become world famous and concentrates on human relations in the family, the work group, and organizations.

A parallel growth took place in Canada, Australia, and New Zealand. Canada, with some apparent reluctance, allowed itself to be much influenced by American sociology and has built many new departments with sociologists trained in the United States.

To a considerable extent Scandinavia and the Netherlands have also adopted the methods and some of the content of American sociology, and the subject has developed rapidly at universities and research institutes. There is also a considerable exchange between sociologists in these countries because their works are typically published regionally as well as in the United Kingdom, the United States, and Germany.

Japanese interest in sociology dates back to the 1870s. The Japanese Sociological Society (Nippon Shakai Gakkai), headquartered at the University of Tokyo, was founded in 1923; by 1960 there were about 150 universities and colleges with courses in the subject. In the early period sociology was nearly all imported; Comte and Spencer, and later Giddings and Gabriel Tarde, were the most influential theorists. After World War II there were rapid changes in sociology in Japan, with empirical research methods largely replacing the earlier philosophical approach. Importations from American sociology were abundant. Popular among these were industrial sociology, social stratification, educational sociology, public opinion research, and the study of mass communication.

Sociology in the former Soviet Union was long held back by the perceived incompatibility of the subject with Marxist theory. Eventually it was permitted to develop, and the number of sociological institutes and chairs of sociology increased. By 1970 the Soviet Sociological Association had more than a thousand members. Leading research interests included labour productivity, education, crime, and alcoholism. Soviet sociology generally avoided issues that might have implied conflict with Marxist thought, concentrating for a time on demography and time-budget studies.

The nations of the Soviet bloc were also periodically inhospitable to sociology, but the strong interest of younger scholars alleviated some of this opposition, and in the second half of the 20th century sociology made considerable progress in Hungary, Poland, the Czech Republic, and Slovakia.

In Israel the dominant department of sociology is at the Hebrew University in Jerusalem, where there are also several research institutes. Departments were also established at the University of Haifa and Tel Aviv University. Israeli sociology maintains continuous close contacts with American sociology, and many of the leading Israeli sociologists have trained or taught in the United States. Among the specialties of Israeli sociology are research in methodology, communication, and criminology. Similarly prominent is the study of collective settlements (kibbutzim), in which new forms of custom and social organization are observed as they develop. Studies of stratification and the labour market have also explored the inequality between Israelis and Arabs.

In Italy, interest in sociology developed in the mid-20th century at several universities, and academic chairs and research institutes gradually increased. Of particular interest to Italian sociology are studies of industrial efficiency, social movements, and social mobility. The model of centralized control over universities, however, has hindered the development of the discipline, both in Italy and in Spain.

In Latin America objective sociology was long resisted, partly because it was viewed as a threat to the political and social order but also because of meagre financial support for research and the low salary level of professors, many of whom were forced to supplement their earnings by engaging in other occupations. In the 1960s, however, the number of full-time chairs increased, and a number of research institutes, some financed by U.S. funds, were established. Political instability in some countries remains a major hindrance, and in such countries able scholars continue to be forced from their university positions from time to time.

Little by little, sociology has penetrated some of the less-developed nations. A number of African universities have formed departments, and the subject is gaining in importance in the Philippines, India, Indonesia, and Pakistan. Some of the more significant developments have occurred in India, where a number of important research institutes have been established.

SCIENTIFIC STATUS

Sociology has not achieved triumphs comparable to those of the older and more heavily supported sciences. Several interpretations have been offered to explain the difference—most frequently, that the growth of sociological knowledge is more random than cumulative. Yet, in some parts of the discipline—such as methodology, human ecology, demography, social differentiation and mobility, attitude research, small-group interaction, public opinion, and mass communication—a slow but significant accumulation of organized and tested knowledge has taken hold. By comparison, some other fields lack this expanding volume of literature. Still, the slow development of published sociological research may stem from a variety of factors: excess use of jargon, a disposition for pseudoquantification, excessive imitation of natural science methodology, and overdependence on interview data, questionnaires, or informal observations. Contemporary sociology is indeed marked by all these shortcomings, but in general there has been progress toward clearer communication and improved methodology, both of which yield more reliable data. As a result, conclusions are drawn from research methods applied to replicated studies that are, in turn, less dependent on the strength of one particular methodological device.

Bias is sometimes presumed to be a chronic affliction of sociology. This may arise in part from the fact that the subject matter of sociology is familiar and important in everyone's daily life. As a result, variations in philosophical outlook and individual preferences can contribute to an irrational bias. Thus, critics have expressed disapproval of the sociologists' skepticism on various matters of faith, of their amoral relativism concerning customs, of their apparent oversimplifications of some principles, and of their particular fashions in categorization and abstraction. But skepticism toward much of the content of folk knowledge is a characteristic of all science, and relativism can be interpreted as merely an avoidance of antiscientific ethnocentrism. Furthermore, abstraction, categorization, and simplification are necessary to the advancement of knowledge, and no one system satisfies everyone.

The dispute about the main purpose of sociology—whether it works to understand behaviour or to cause social change—is a dispute found in every pursuit of scientific knowledge, and such polarization is far from absolute. Scholars differ in the degree to which they regard the value of science as an intellectual understanding of the cosmos or as an instrument for immediate improvement of the human lot. Since even the "purest" scientist conceives of his work as benefiting mankind, the issue narrows to a difference in preference between an ad hoc attack on immediate human problems and a long-run trust that basic knowledge, gathered without reference to present urgencies, is even more valuable. In some countries there is much pressure toward early practicality of results; in others, including the United States, the larger number of scholars and the principal sociological associations have shown preference for "basic science."

A degree of polarization has also arisen over the proper strategy for research—whether research should take its direction from the needs of society and humankind or from the evolving theoretical corpus of sociology. In nations that allow academic freedom, such disputes are usually

ROBERT PARK

A leading figure in what came to be known as the "Chicago school" of sociology, Robert E. Park (1864–1944) was noted for his work on ethnic minority groups, particularly African Americans, and on human ecology, a term he is credited with coining. Park's graduate work was done after 11 years of experience as a newspaper reporter in various large cities, where his interest in social problems was stimulated. He earned degrees at the University of Michigan, Harvard University, and the University of Heidelberg and taught at Harvard, the University of Chicago, and Fisk University.

In 1906 Park wrote two magazine articles about the oppression of the Congolese by Belgian colonial administrators. He became secretary to Booker T. Washington and is said to have written most of Washington's "The Man Farthest Down" (1912). Park believed that a caste system produced by sharp ethnic differences tends, because of the division of labour between the castes, to change into a structure of economic classes.

With Ernest W. Burgess, Park wrote a standard text, "Introduction to the Science of Sociology" (1921). Three volumes of his "Collected Papers" were published between 1950 and 1955.

of low intensity because scholars select research interests on any basis they prefer, including that of personal taste. In this way presumably the motivation of the investigator is maximized.

Sociologists most interested in action express impatience at the claims of others who prefer to separate their research from personal values. Much of the dispute prevails only because the two sides argue past each other. There can be wide agreement that no human being is without personal values, that research forced to confirm a particular set of values is not good science, and that there can be scientific issues toward which a particular investigator is value-neutral. In research that is susceptible to contamination by the values of the worker, it is generally possible to minimize the damage by employing methodological devices that prevent the researcher from imposing his or her wishes on a particular outcome. These devices include objective observational techniques, measurement methods, and independent or blind analysis of results.

CURRENT TRENDS

Sociology will continue to grow in the foreseeable future. Among present trends contributing to this growth are the increase in public appreciation of the subject, the continuing growth of funds for teaching and research, the steady reduction of sectarian opposition to study of social institutions, the refinement of methodologies that permit statistical analysis, and the growth of acceptance from scientists in other fields. Although factors such as extreme nationalism and internal conflict can inhibit growth in sociology, such conditions have impeded development only locally and temporarily.

Furthermore, it appears likely that public interest in the development of sociological knowledge will increase as more people come to realize what sociology can contribute to human safety and welfare. Advances in science and technology will always be accompanied by unforeseen and unintended consequences. Progress can indeed diminish the effects of natural catastrophes such as famine and disease, but progress can also bring about a wide range of new problems. These are not the menaces of an impersonal nature but dangers that arise from imperfection in human behaviour, particularly in organized human relations. In addition, wars have shown a tendency to become larger and ever more destructive, and the causes, though far from being understood, clearly lie, in large measure, in the complexities of social organization, in the interaction of great corporate national bodies. It can be argued that politics, unaided by social science and other disciplines, cannot reverse this trend.

Problems within nations are seen as increasing sources of human troubles. There is a general rise in the severity of ethnic hostilities and of internal conflicts between generations, political factions, and other divisions of the populations. Human welfare is also threatened by widespread poverty, crime, vice, political corruption, and breakdowns in the family and in other institutions. Contemporary sociology does not yet provide the solutions, but its practitioners believe that the prospects for human betterment depend in large part on the increasing application of social science knowledge to these enduring problems.

Applications of sociology also appear to be spreading in several directions. Many sociologists are employed by national and international bodies to recommend programs, evaluate their progress and effects, gather data for planning, and propose methods for initiating change. Sociologists aid industry by obtaining data on clients and workers. Some of this work includes social surveys, offering advice on personnel or public relations problems, providing labour unions with advice, helping communities undertake reform, counseling families, and donating or selling advice to consumer groups. As long as organizations need information on their various publics, there will be strong demand for sociological knowledge.

Progress into the deeper sociological questions will require greater resources, larger research teams, and special research agencies. This compares to the increased complexity of research organization that occurred in the older sciences. In addition, large-scale sociological research will continue to be enhanced by the availability of computers and the Internet and by the use of complex statistical techniques.

The study of sociology can be applied to a broad spectrum of careers in a variety of locations.

EMERGING ROLES FOR SOCIOLOGISTS

The principal employment of sociologists has been in academic institutions, but other employment possibilities have opened in recent decades. Social welfare agencies have long employed sociologists, and government organizations of all types—from bureaus dealing with population, budgets, and education to departments concentrating on crime, agriculture, and health matters—have tapped sociologists for help in research, planning, and administration. Other directions of sociological activity include the roles of consultant, social critic, social activist, and even revolutionary. When the activity diverges far enough from true scholarship and traditional academic sociology, it may cease to be regarded as sociological, but it appears likely that sociologists will continue to spread their activities over an ever-widening region of national or global concern

CONCLUSION

When Auguste Comte coined the term "sociology," it meant for him a comprehensive science of humanity. He and writers who shared his views took all civilization as their subject. Other sociologists of the 19th century were more interested in the immediate social problems they witnessed growing around them—poverty, squalor, broken families, child labor, and other by-products of the factory system. These sociologists saw the same problems about which Socialists and Communists were complaining, but they approached solutions from a different angle. The sociologists were not necessarily revolutionaries, as was Friedrich Engels, author of *The Condition of the Working Class in England in 1844* (1845). In volume two of *Democracy in America* (1840), Alexis de Tocqueville gave an extended account of the manners, customs, and social institutions of Americans.

Today sociology is the study of how humans behave in social groups with an interest in patterns of social relationships and interactions. It looks at customs, traditions, and social institutions such as the family, marriage, and the educational system. While the family is one of the smallest social groups, sociologists also look at such institutions as government and how particular governments interact with each other and with global institutions. As we have seen, sociology is closely tied to the other sciences under the social sciences umbrella, and its applications are far-reaching.

GLOSSARY

ACHIEVED SOCIAL STATUS Status that is achieved, requiring special qualities and gained through competition and individual effort.

ASCRIBED SOCIAL STATUS Status that is assigned to individuals at birth without reference to any innate abilities.

BIAS Systematic error introduced into sampling or testing by selecting or encouraging one outcome or answer over others.

DEMOGRAPHY The statistical study of human populations especially with reference to size and density, distribution, and vital statistics.

ECOLOGICAL PATTERNING Methodology of urban research that involves mapping locations.

ECONOMIC DETERMINISM The Marxist idea that social differentiation and class conflict result from economic factors.

EMPIRICISM The practice of basing ideas and theories on testing and experience.

ETHNOMETHODOLOGY The study of people's commonsense understandings of the structure of social interaction.

FUNCTIONALISM A theory that stresses the interdependence of the patterns and institutions of a society and their interaction in maintaining cultural and social unity.

HUMAN ECOLOGY A branch of sociology dealing especially with the spatial and temporal interrelationships between humans and their economic, social, and political organization.

INDIVIDUALISM A political and social philosophy that emphasizes the moral worth of the individual.

INTERACTIONISM Theory that all one's perceptions of and reactions to the external world are mediated or influenced by prior ideas, valuations, and assessments.

LAISSEZ-FAIRE A philosophy or practice characterized by a usually deliberate abstention from direction or interference especially with individual freedom of choice and action.

METHODOLOGY The set of principles or procedures of inquiry in a particular field; also, the study of such principles or procedures.

POSITIVISM The theory that positive knowledge is based on natural phenomena and their properties and relations as verified by the empirical sciences.

SOCIAL CHANGE The alteration of mechanisms within the social structure, characterized by changes in cultural symbols, rules of behaviour, social organizations, or value systems.

SOCIAL CLASS A group of people within a society who possess roughly the same socioeconomic status.

SOCIAL NORM A rule or standard of behaviour shared by members of a social group.

SOCIAL SCIENCE A branch of science that deals with the institutions and functioning of human society and with the interpersonal relationships of individuals as members of society.

SOCIAL STATUS The relative rank that an individual holds, with attendant rights, duties, and lifestyle, in a social hierarchy based upon honour or prestige.

SOCIAL STRUCTURE The regular and repetitive aspects of the interactions between the members of a given social entity.

SOCIETY Community life thought of as a system within which the individual lives.

SOCIOLOGY The systematic study of the development, structure, interaction, and collective behaviour of organized groups of human beings.

SOCIOMETRY The measurement techniques used in social psychology, in sociology, and sometimes in social anthropology and psychiatry based on the assessment of social choice and interpersonal attractiveness.

STRATIFICATION The state of being divided into social classes.

STRUCTURALISM Theory that contends that no social element can be examined or explained outside its context or the pattern or structure of which it is a part.

BIBLIOGRAPHY

Among older titles of major significance, generally considered classics, are William Graham Sumner, *Folkways* (1906, reissued 1992); Charles Horton Cooley, *Human Nature and the Social Order* (1902, reprinted 1983); George H. Mead, *Mind, Self, & Society from the Standpoint of a Social Behaviorist*, ed. by Charles W. Morris (1934, reissued 1990); Ellsworth Faris, *The Nature of Human Nature, and Other Essays in Social Psychology* (1937, reissued 1972), also published in an abridged ed. with the same title (1976); Robert E. Park and Ernest W. Burgess, *Introduction to the Science of Sociology*, 3rd ed. rev. (1972), also published in an abridged ed. with the same title (1970); and William Fielding Ogburn, *Social Change with Respect to Culture and Original Nature*, new ed. (1950, reissued 1966). A comprehensive summary of early sociological theory is available in Harry Elmer Barnes (ed.), *An Introduction to the History of Sociology* (1948, reissued 1961), also published in an abridged ed. with the same title (1966). Later developments are found in Roscoe C. Hinkle, *Founding Theory of American Sociology, 1881–1915* (1980), and *Developments in American Sociological Theory, 1915–1950* (1994); and Anthony Giddens, *Social Theory and Modern Sociology* (1987). The following titles provide excellent coverage of the main directions and subfields of contemporary sociology: Robert E.L. Faris (ed.), *Handbook of Modern Sociology* (1964, reissued 1968); Robert K. Merton, Leonard Broom, and Leonard S. Cottrell, Jr. (eds.), *Sociology Today*, 2 vol. (1959, reissued 1965); Georges Gurvitch and Wilbert E. Moore (eds.), *Twentieth Century Sociology* (1945); James G. March (ed.), *Handbook of Organizations* (1965, reprinted in 2 vol., 1987); Howard W. Odum, *American Sociology* (1951, reissued 1969); Neil J. Smelser (ed.), *Handbook of Sociology* (1988); Stephen Park Turner and Jonathan H. Turner, *The Impossible Science: An Institutional Analysis of American Sociology* (1990); Randall Collins, *Theoretical Sociology* (1988); and Edgar F. Borgotta (ed.), *Encyclopedia of Sociology*, 4 vol., 2nd ed. (2000). Leading books treating communities and societies as wholes are Talcott Parsons, *Societies: Evolutionary and Comparative Perspectives* (1966); Robert K. Merton, *Social Theory and Social Structure*, enlarged ed. (1968); Patrick Nolan and

Gerhard Lenski, *Human Societies: An Introduction to Macrosociology*, 8th ed. (1999); and Arthur L. Stinchcombe, *Constructing Social Theories* (1968, reprinted 1987). The technical and statistical methods used in sociology are presented in Royce A. Singleton, Jr., and Bruce C. Straits, *Approaches to Social Research*, 3rd ed. (1999); and George W. Bohrnstedt and David Knoke, *Statistics for Social Data Analysis,* 3rd ed. (1994).

INDEX

A

Adorno, T.W., 82
Althusser, Louis, 83
American Journal of Sociology, 119, 120, 122
American Occupational Structure, The, 86
Ancient Society, 54

B

Bagehot, Walter, 57
Benjamin, Walter, 82
Blau, Peter, 86
Burgess, Ernest, 100, 106, 129

C

castes, 14, 33–34, 129
"charismatic leadership," 39–40
Chicago School, 48, 74, 84, 97, 106, 129
class, theories of, 77, 79–80
Coleman, James S., 96–97, 98–99
"Communist Manifesto, The" 59–60
Comte, Auguste, 10–11, 12, 15–16, 36, 39, 42–45, 47, 104, 118, 123, 125, 134
conflict theory, 35, 76, 84
Cooley, Charles, 7, 8, 97
Coser, Lewis, 84
Cours de philosophie positive, 11
critical theory, 82, 83, 84
cultural theory, 69
culture, establishing definition of, 52
"culture of poverty," 94–95

D

Darwin, Charles, 11, 12, 49, 50, 53, 56, 110
data collection, protocols for, 114–115
"deep structures," 80, 83
demography, 108–110
developmentalism, 21–22
Duncan, Otis Dudley, 86
Durkheim, Émile, 8, 16, 30–31, 37, 47, 70, 73, 77, 78, 102, 103, 104, 123

E

ecological patterning, 106, 108–110
economic determinism, 59–61
electorate, broadening of as theme of social sciences, 8–19
Elias, Norbert, 40
Engels, Friedrich, 39, 54, 134
Essay on the Principle of Population, An, 4
ethnomethodology, 100

evolution, as influence on social sciences, 10, 11–12, 21–22, 36–37, 39, 47–50, 52–53, 54
experimental methods, 64, 68, 69, 110–111

F

factory system, as theme of social sciences, 8
First Principles, 49
Foucault, Michel, 83
Foundations of Social Theory, 96–97
Frankfurt School, 82–83, 84
Freudianism, 19–20
Fromm, Erich, 82
functionalism
  early, 70–72, 74
  overview of, 23–24
functionalist-conflict debate, 74–76, 84, 85

G

Garfinkel, Harold, 100
Gemeinschaft, social systems and, 71
Gesellschaft, social systems and, 71
Giddings, Franklin H., 118, 125
Goffman, Erving, 100
Graunt, John, 108

H

Habermas, Jürgen, 83
Hindus, caste and, 33–34, 35
Hobhouse, Leonard, 47, 56, 124
Horkheimer, Max, 82, 123
human ecology, 61–63
humanitarianism, as influence on social sciences, 10, 11
Hunter, Floyd, 86, 89

I

individualism, 50, 51–52
Institute for Social Research, 82, 123
interactionism, 24
interdisciplinary approaches, sociology and, 20–21, 95–97

K

Kerr, Clark, 39
kinship, social structure and, 29

L

labour
  division of and social structure, 29
  as theme of social sciences, 6
language, social structure and, 29
"law of three stages," 36, 39, 44–45

Lenski, Gerhard, 86–87, 89
Lévi-Strauss, Claude, 80, 83
Lewin, Kurt, 110
"logic of industrialization," 39
"looking glass self," 7
Lynd, Helen, 85–86, 89
Lynd, Robert, 85–86, 89

M

Malinowski, Bronislaw, 71–72
Malthus, Thomas, 4–6, 46, 47
Marcuse, Herbert, 82, 83
Martineau, Harriet, 45–46
Marx, Karl, 8, 12, 19, 20, 39, 54, 59–61, 79, 89, 93, 91, 104, 119
Marxism, 18–19, 35, 39, 54, 59–61, 76, 79–80, 82, 89, 93, 116, 125, 126
Merton, Robert K., 74, 77
Middletown studies, 85–86
Mills, C. Wright, 86, 87
Moreno, J.L., 112, 113
Morgan, Lewis Henry, 47, 54
Murdock, George P., 31

O

Odum, Howard, 106, 109
Ogburn, William Fielding, 106, 107, 109
On the Origin of Species, 11, 12

P

Park, Robert, 8, 100, 106, 129
Parsons, Talcott, 74, 77, 78–79, 96
Pearson, Karl, 111, 112
Play, Frédéric Le, 8, 16, 102
Polish Peasant in Europe and America, 104, 105
population growth, as theme of social sciences, 4–6
positivism, as influence on social sciences, 10, 43–44
power, theories of, 77, 79–80
Power and Privilege, 86
"power elite," 86, 87
Presentation of Self in Everyday Life, The, 100
Primitive Culture, 50, 52–53
property, transformation of as theme of social sciences, 6

Q

Quetelet, Adolphe, 8

R

Radcliffe-Brown, A.R., 76, 77
Recent Social Trends in the United States, 106, 109
reform movements, 28
revolutionary movements, 28

rising expectations, as major theme of 20th century sociology, 17–18

S

Saussure, Ferdinand de, 80
Simmel, George, 8, 16, 123
Small, Albion, 48, 118, 119
social change
  explanations of, 38–41
  overview of, 35–38
social class, 90–91, 93–95
social Darwinism, 7, 36–37, 47–50, 56–58, 59
socialization, study of in social psychology, 67–68
social movements, overview of, 28
social psychology, 14–15, 19, 63–69
social sciences, 19th century
  major themes, 3–6, 8–10
  methodological developments, 102–104
  new movements, 10–12
  origins, 1–3
    sociology as separate discipline, 12–17
  what it is, 1
social sciences, 20th century
  Freudianism and, 19–20
    interdisciplinary approaches, 20–21
  major theories, 21–24
  Marxism and, 18–19
  overview, 17–18
  specialization, 20
Social Statics, 49
social status, 31–35
social stratification, 85–90
social-systems theories, 22–23
society and social structure
  overview of, 26–27, 29
  and social organization, 30–31
sociology, contemporary
  academic status, 118, 120–127
  current trends, 130–1331
  methodological developments, 104, 106–117
  national preferences in methodology, 64, 115–117
  new roles for sociologists, 133
  scientific status, 127–130
  segmentation of the discipline, 84
  what it is, 25–26
sociometry, 66, 113, 112
Spencer, Herbert, 12, 15–16, 36–37, 47, 48–50, 57, 102, 124
statistical and mathematical analysis, 111–112, 114
status groups, 33, 35
structural functionalism, 35, 74, 76–77, 79
structuralism, 23, 24, 80, 83–84
structural linguistics, 80
Structure of Social Action, 78
Suicide, 73, 102, 103
Sumner, William Graham, 57
symbolic interaction theory, 97–98, 100

T

technology, as theme of social sciences, 8
Thomas, W.I., 104, 105
Tilly, Charles, 40, 95
Tocqueville, Alexis de, 8, 16, 134
Tönnies, Ferdinand, 8, 16, 71, 123
Truly Disadvantaged, The, 89, 92
Tylor, E.B., 47, 50, 52–54

U

urbanization, as theme of social sciences, 6, 8

V

violence
  relation to social structure, 29
  and social change, 40–41

W

Warner, W. Lloyd, 86, 89
Weber, Max, 8, 16, 37, 39, 61, 78, 87, 93–94, 123
Wilson, William Julius, 89, 92–93
Wirth, Louis, 120, 122

Z

Znaniecki, Florian, 14, 105